The Community
Economic Base Study

BY CHARLES M. TIEBOUT

*Professor of Economics
and Business Administration
University of Washington*

December, 1962

Supplementary Paper No. 16
Published by the
COMMITTEE FOR ECONOMIC DEVELOPMENT

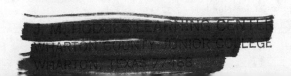

AREA DEVELOPMENT ADVISORY BOARD

Contents

Foreword

The first CED policy statement directed specifically towards assisting communities to provide for more efficient allocation of public and private resources, *Guiding Metropolitan Growth*, said that an understanding of the local economy was essential to development of sound local public policy. "The proper starting point is the realization that a community is a place for earning a living. Population settles or expands primarily because of job opportunities. Private investment occurs because of income-earning opportunities. The daily movement of people is largely a result of job requirements. The development of public capital improvements and services occurs to a considerable extent to assist the economic activities of the area."

An economic base study is a method of examining the local economy to bring about the necessary understanding of how a community earns its living. There have been many such studies over the past three decades, some good, some quite misleading. A sound study must organize an adequate amount of information into a logical structure that corresponds to the realities of economic life. Yet the funds to support such studies and the number of people trained to make them are limited.

There has long been a need for a single small volume which brings together the best thinking on the logic of base studies and emphasizes methods which are within the financial and technical means of most communities. Such a study should be of service to many businessmen, civic leaders, government officials, and scholars. With this purpose in mind the Area Development Committee of CED sponsored Professor Tiebout's efforts to prepare such a report and is happy to publish it.

The Area Development Committee wishes to thank the many scholars, businessmen and officials who have made recommendations which have contributed to the manuscript. As noted elsewhere, Professor Tiebout is entirely responsible for the work.

John H. Nixon
Director of Area Development

Preface and Acknowledgments

In the late thirties the concept of the economic base became a standard tool in the analysis of the local economy. Its development was largely the work of urban geographers, land use analysts, and city planners. In 1940 an article appeared in the *Economic Journal* by M. C. Daly, "An Approximation to a Geographical Multiplier." Those interested in base analysis hardly noticed this piece while for economists it was simply another extension of the newly developed concept of the multiplier. The fact that both concepts are essentially the same went largely unnoticed until the fifties. Indeed, today many economists rebel at the naivete of many base studies. In like manner, non-economists rebel at the seemingly useless jargon such as propensities, induced income, and accelerator affects introduced into base analysis by economists. If the non-economist has overreacted against the intrusion of technical economics, the economist — myself included — has not extended himself in explaining the base concept and relating it to modern income and employment analysis. In this piece I have attempted to explain the economist's view of the base concept. As usual, for exposition some liberties have been taken with economic rigor — none, I trust, too severe.

Some may feel that the base concept presented here is too simple and that it has been replaced by newer more elegant frameworks, such as input-output. At the conceptual level this is in many ways correct. My interest here, however, is not at the conceptual level. It is empirical. And if this piece appears a little too "pro base studies," it is because of their relative empirical simplicity.

One of the delightful by-products of the preparation of this work was the opportunity to communicate with experts in the regional field. Some were old friends upon whom one always imposes manuscripts. Others are new friends who kindly offered criticisms and suggestions.

The following people read the whole or parts of this manuscript and offered many useful suggestions: Miles L. Colean, Jesse Burkhead, Charles Leven, Alfred C. Neal, Herbert Stein, Peter E. de Janosi, W. Lee Hansen, Henry Bruck, Frederick O'R. Hayes, Luther Gulick, Victor Roterus, and Robert Colwell.

Professors W. Lee Hansen of U.C.L.A. and Leland Howell of Drury College tore earlier drafts of this work to shreds and then helped to reassemble the pieces. Messrs. Pierre Crosson, Harold Buma, and Richard Peterson, all of the Economics Department, Bank of America, did the same thing — only more gently, as one would expect of people who work in downtown San Francisco.

The CED Area Development staff has been cooperative in the fullest. Messrs. John Nixon, Donald Gilmore, and Paul Gerhardt and Miss Thelma Palmerio have been most helpful with everything from the broad issues of organization and content to the more particular ones of clarity in exposition. Miss Mavis Saunders, Miss Margery Fitzpatrick, and Mr. Eugene Wagener transformed rough manuscript into typewritten pages adeptly.

With such a long list of able commentators, it might seem that such a book cannot miss. Since this may not be the case, the shortcomings remain the sole property of the author.

Charles M. Tiebout
Seattle, Washington,
October 3, 1962

7

Introduction

The economic base of a community consists of those activities which provide the basic employment and income on which the rest of the local economy depends. An economic base study identifies the basic sources of employment and income and provides an understanding of the source and level of all employment and income in a community. The primary objective of an economic base study is to develop information which will help a community solve local problems, make better decisions about matters that will enlarge economic opportunities for its citizens, improve their welfare, and make it possible for them to increase their contributions to national growth.

This book describes what an economic base study is, explains how communities can profit by such a study, and presents guidelines for conducting this kind of research on a limited budget. It stresses how studies of the economic base provide information needed to make intelligent decisions on a broad range of local issues. This is written primarily for local government officials, planners, urban geographers, persons concerned with industrial development, planning, and urban renewal, realtors, and local leaders and citizens interested in improving the way in which their communities develop and function.

Persons not involved in actually conducting an economic base study will probably be most interested in Part I, which outlines the nature of these studies and their uses without getting into detailed mechanics. Those directly involved in carrying out a base study will be interested in the more technical discussion contained in Part II. It will also help persons using base studies to interpret and evaluate the results. Part II discusses the mechanics of income flows in a community, local economic groupings and how these groupings provide a useful framework to help understand economic interrelationships, theoretical and technical issues involved in economic base studies, criticisms made of base studies, problems involved in carrying them out, and methods of preparing forecasts associated with such studies.

9

Part 1

Guide to Economic Base Studies

Chapter 1

The Importance of Understanding
The Community Economic Base

"The first step toward meeting the public problems of an area is a detailed knowledge of its economic base. Knowledge about the economic base is essential to sound public decisions in the form of master plans, zoning ordinances, transportation plans, renewal programs and other public improvement plans. Public policy towards taxation, distribution of municipal costs and municipal borrowing should take such information into account. Private investment plans call for knowledge of the market prospects in the region."

CED, *Guiding Metropolitan Growth*[1]

The Need for Better Information

A substantial improvement in recent decades in both the quantity and quality of information about the workings of the national economy has greatly improved the quality of decisions made by public officials and by businessmen having to do with the national economy.

At the local level, thousands of decisions are made regularly by public officials and by businessmen. In the aggregate, these decisions have a great impact on economic growth and the quality of living standards of the American

---

[1] A Statement on National Policy by the Research and Policy Committee of CED, August 1960.

people. Yet, such decisions are usually based on much less detailed economic information than is available at the national level. A regular flow of sound economic information about each local economy and its economic base would contribute to the quality of decisions made at the local level by public officials and business leaders.

Additional local information can be most helpful if it is:

1. Gathered and reported at periodic intervals;
2. Related to national statistics on employment, income and industrial production;
3. Organized around sound concepts of the working of the local economy, so that information on the interrelations of various types of activity can be understood.

Guiding Metropolitan Growth suggested ten questions to which studies at the local level might be directed to provide information needed as a basis for better informed public and private decisions. These questions fall into three groups:

A. *The Sources of Current Income and Employment*
1. What have been the precise sources of employment, income and output in the past?
2. Which of these sources have served markets outside the metropolitan area and will be affected by external markets?
3. Which have served markets within the metropolitan area?

The first three questions relate to the present structure of a local economy. Answers to these will help in answering questions four through seven which deal with possible future levels of activity.

B. *The Prospects for Economic Growth or Decline*
4. What are the prospects for future growth, change or decline in those various economic activities? What new industries may be expected to emerge within the next decade or two?
5. How does public policy influence the growth, change or decline of various economic activities?
6. What change may be expected in the size and mix of the labor force?
7. To what extent will labor services be supplied by residents of the region or by new migrants?

The final three questions begin to probe vital questions concerning patterns of development within sections of a community.

C. *Relationship of Land Use and Community Services to Economic Growth or Decline*
8. What are the residential preferences of high and middle-income families? And how and where are the housing needs of low-income people likely to be met?
9. What kinds of community and institutional facilities are required at current or anticipated levels of services?
10. In view of these factors, what are the likely uses of different districts and neighborhoods within the region?

This booklet describes methods to answer the first three questions and suggests techniques to deal with the fourth. It also indicates how periodic economic base studies supply useful information for answering the remaining questions. Questions two and three recognize that ours is an economy of specialization and exchange. Every community in the United States purchases goods and services from outside its borders. A community pays for these goods and services by specializing in the production of certain goods and services which it sells outside the community. The goods and services sold outside the community play a key role in determining the economic health of the community.

Economic Base Studies in Brief

An economic base study identifies the key economic activities of the community. Base studies begin by defining the community to be studied: a municipality, county, metropolitan area, marketing area, or some other geographic unit. Next, as questions two and three in *Guiding Metropolitan Growth* suggest, economic base studies divide the local economy into two segments: (1) firms and individuals serving markets outside the community; and (2) firms and individuals serving markets within the community.

The goods and services which the community sells outside its boundaries are considered exports. Exports include all sales made outside the community, not just trade with foreign nations. The remaining goods and services go to the local market. Local is defined to mean the geographic region being studied.

Implicit in this division of markets is the cause and effect relationship. Export markets are considered the prime mover of the local economy. If employment serving this market rises or falls, employment serving the local market is presumed to move in the same direction. When the factory (export) closes, retail merchants (local) feel the impact as laid-off factory workers have less to spend. Because of this prime mover role export employment is considered as "basic." Employment which serves the local market is considered adaptive and is titled "non-basic."[2]

Economic base analysis recognizes that industries, and firms within industries, may sell their products in both markets. For example, the local breweries may sell to both export and local markets. Thus, employment at the breweries is partly basic and partly non-basic. For each industry in the community, employment is placed in the basic or non-basic category or divided between the two. Then totals are added up for both basic and non-basic employment.

How much non-basic employment will be created if basic employment increases? The simplest assumption is that over the long run the proportion of basic and non-basic jobs will remain about the same. Hence, an increase in the number of basic jobs will eventually produce a proportionate increase in non-basic jobs. For example, in a community with total employment of 100,000, suppose that 40,000 is basic and 60,000 non-basic employment. What happens to total employ-

---

[2] Sometimes other labels are used for export employment, such as city-founding, primary, and foundation. Terms often used to describe non-basic employment include city-filling, secondary and residentary.

ment if a new plant opens in the community and increases basic employment by 400 jobs? In the long run non-basic employment will also rise to supply the new demands of the additional work force. Assuming proportionality, for every four basic jobs, six non-basic jobs will be created. Thus, total employment will rise by 1,000, the 400 basic jobs to begin with plus the additional 600 non-basic jobs.[3]

One important use of a base study is in making some kind of forecast, although a forecast is not necessarily part of a base study.[4] When the economic forces which have made the community what it is are understood, it is easier to project how these and other economic forces will affect the community in the future. First, the growth or decline of employment in basic industries is forecast for some time period. Then associated non-basic employment growth or decline can be determined. These projections can help greatly in forecasting changes in population, income, land use and the tax base. Forecasts of trends in these fields, in turn, can be used in planning to meet a wide range of public and private needs of the area, such as in planning and zoning, capital budgeting, taxes and expenditures, housing, transportation, electric, gas, telephone and other utility services as well as needs for many other services.

This brief description suggests in generalities what base studies are all about.[5] While the general notion may be easy to grasp, a number of assumptions and qualifications have been omitted. Part II goes into the empirical and technical issues in more detail and suggests methods of carrying out such studies.

---

[3] Those familiar with economic base studies will note that there is no reference to the use of base studies in the short run and much over-simplification for long-run analysis. Refinements are introduced in Part II.

[4] Forecasting methods are discussed in more detail in Part II, Chapters 6 and 7.

[5] There is one type of study which may have come to the reader's attention as an alternative for an economic base study, a community input-output study. At a purely formal-theoretical level an input-output study can provide all of the information given by a base study. When it comes to the ease of empirical implementation, input-output studies require substantially more detailed data, much of which must be developed by extensive surveys. Thus larger research budgets are necessary. Further, they are more applicable to large regions where economic interrelations are more complex.

Chapter 2

The Uses of a Base Study

The uses of a base study are numerous. Some of them can be suggested here. Others are better appreciated after the discussion in Part II. An economic base study can help business firms and government bodies meet present and future problems. Frequently base studies also provide the necessary background for more specialized studies. Thus, base studies lead to or are often coupled with research into marketing, urban renewal, land use, transportation, water supply, and similar fields of special interest.

This chapter illustrates some of the uses of a base study in and of itself, as an aid in forecasting and, finally, as an integral part of other studies of special problems.

Direct Benefits of a Base Study

The *general information* provided by an economic base study is valuable to businessmen, civic leaders, government officials, planners, educators and development groups. The following are examples of specific benefits:

1. Base studies provide an understanding of the current sources of income and employment.

   Example: In some communities seemingly small industries may be revealed as a major source of basic employment.

2. Base studies can pinpoint weaknesses in the community's economy.

   Example: How much of the export employment is tied to one industry?

3. As an aid in economic education, base studies are extremely worthwhile.

   Example: Base studies made available to high schools provide a useful aid in teaching economics. Students can understand general economic principles more easily if they are related to familiar situations in their community.

4. Information resulting from an economic base study assists in making governmental decisions.

   Example: Since the "business climate" depends largely on the attractiveness of the community to export concerns, government officials need to know whether present local taxes are relatively heavier on export industries than on locally-oriented industries.

Periodic base studies can enable a community to evaluate its progress toward certain broad public goals. These would include: (1) increasing total income and employment; (2) increasing per capita income; (3) attaining reasonable cyclical stability; (4) maintaining healthy prospects for future growth. Per capita income provides a measure of the average citizen's well-being. Base studies carried on over time will measure changes in per capita income and help

15

to unearth the reasons for such changes. Cyclical stability implies that employment and income in a community are not subject to extreme swings over a business cycle. A base study points out the industrial mix of the export industries. If this mix of industries is highly sensitive to cyclical fluctuations, then encouragement of more stable industries is suggested as an appropriate policy objective.

A base study is valuable both to business firms located outside the community and those located within the community.

Outside firms looking for information on local market potential will find useful information in a community base study. The local market for a particular product may justify establishment of a branch plant. A base study may indicate whether the market is ready now or at what future time the market may be ready. (Determination of whether a product could be produced locally will also require information on costs and revenues which a base study alone would not provide.)

For firms already established in a community a base study helps trace the local sources of demand for their products and services. It indicates the relation of the fortunes of the firm to the other parts of the local economy. Even local firms selling largely in regional and national markets will find a base study valuable because it describes the factors in the local economy which influence their costs.

Base Studies as an Aid in Forecasting

The previous chapter mentioned briefly how a base study can help in forecasting community economic growth. Here this point is elaborated a bit. The main details are left to Chapter 7 in Part II.

Forecasts can run a wide range from a simple projection of trends to complex formulations such as those made for the New York Regional Study.[1] An essential step in forecasting is the identification of key factors which are important to future levels of activity. For example, in forecasting national income for the coming year, surveys of business plans for capital expenditure provide valuable information.

For communities the key factor is the basic or export market. How will it grow or decline over the next decade? As the basic market changes so too will the non-basic market. In essence, base analysis concentrates much of the forecaster's task. Detailed attention needs to be paid primarily to the export market. To be sure, this is task enough and Part II warns against any simple application of basic/non-basic ratios. Nevertheless, base studies, by identifying the current export industries, provide a useful first step in forecasting.

Forecasts of community prospects rest largely on economic analysis. But what if demographic and population studies indicate a smaller labor force than the forecasted total employment? This kind of a cross check indicates that something is amiss. Perhaps the net in-migration has been too conservatively estimated, and the community should plan for a larger number of new residents. A different problem arises if projections of labor force skills indicate a surplus of workers for a particular industry. Unless community action, such as a training

---

[1] See Barbara Berman, Benjamin Chinitz, and Edgar Hoover, *Projection of a Metropolis,* Cambridge: Harvard University Press, 1960.

16

program, is undertaken, structural unemployment may result.

Over a long period an economic base study can play a useful role in efforts to develop job opportunities. This is recognized by the Area Redevelopment Administration of the U. S. Department of Commerce which is charged with the task of aiding redevelopment areas in the nation. As part of their program they require that communities prepare an Over-all Economic Development Program, popularly known as the OEDP. They note that:

> The OEDP may be broader than an economic base study (especially in the OEDP's recommended program phases), but the OEDP should include much of the data and analysis common to such studies and useful in program formulation.[2]

Thus, a base study with a forecast is considered an essential part of a program of economic development.

Base Studies Used in Conjunction With Other Studies

Base studies most frequently appear coupled to other studies of specific problems. In this section base studies are shown to be useful in dealing with over-all land use planning, transportation planning, estimating future governmental revenues and expenditures, and solving problems associated with the community's ability to supply goods at a competitive price.

Perhaps the most frequent use of an economic base study comes as an aid in *land use planning*. It is often the local planning agency which undertakes an economic base study in conjunction with a land use study. Community planning is concerned with spatial allocation of activities within the community. The interest is in patterns of growth. Patterns imply groups or aggregates, such as heavy manufacturing, light manufacturing, transportation, retail-commercial, service-commercial, multi-family residential and single-family residential uses. The first use of an economic base study in planning is to help provide "control totals" for these aggregates. Let's see what this implies.

The planning process involves allocating totals of various kinds of uses within a given land area. For example, what will be the volume of retail activity and what will its space requirements be? A base study with a projection can help to answer such questions. Traditionally the steps involved, omitting complications, can be summarized as follows:

1. Forecast export employment for the year, say 1980. Suppose this amounts to some 333,000 jobs.
2. Via the base/non-base analysis estimate the local employment, say 667,000 jobs.
3. Estimate the land use requirements — square feet per worker or some such unit — in the various export and locally oriented industries.
4. With the aid of other studies allocate this land within the community.
5. See if these land requirements can be met with available sites and under present zoning regulations. Also how do these land require-

[2] Area Redevelopment Administration U. S. Department of Commerce, *The Over-all Economic Development Program*, August, 1961, p. 7.

ments match those specified in the comprehensive (master) plan, especially with respect to transportation plans and the need for public facilities.

Even though the steps are highly summarized, the reader can see the underlying procedure and benefits.

The relation of base studies to *transportation planning* is important, but the connection is less apparent. Most transportation studies begin with an over-all projection of economic levels. They also develop information on the expected industrial structure. Again, control totals are necessary. Trips generated depend on many factors. One of the important factors is the level and type of industrial activity. A base study and an associated forecast are important in projecting such factors.

Base studies with projections are an aid in planning *governmental capital expenditure needs* and *expected revenues*. Failure to make accurate projections for major capital expenditures can lead to over- and under-investment by the public. In a Western region, for example, the provision of water was an important topic, and on this subject a great deal of analysis was made. Yet, fundamental to the study and discussion was an economic analysis of the whole region and a projection of its future needs. This constituted less than one per cent of the total discussion in one of the major reports. If the future does not produce the economic boom forecast for the area, the voters will be saddled with a large bonded indebtedness to provide water they will not need.

Long-term estimates of capital needs generally are accompanied by long-term estimates of service requirements — the demand for school teachers, policemen and firemen, welfare payments, and other public servants or public services. Public capital expenditures and services must be paid for generally from public revenues. At the local level the most important source of revenue is the property tax. In many localities the property tax is one of the few taxes with revenue yields which are fairly fixed. This, of course, is true only in the short run. In the long run, revenues from the property tax not only depend upon tax rates, but the tax base as well. If the community fails to grow, the tax base will not expand. Forecasts associated with a base study help estimate the future tax base and property tax yield.

Receipts from many other local taxes vary more immediately with the level of economic activity. By way of example, consider the sales tax. Given the rate and the coverage, the revenue depends upon the amount of local sales. An economic base study using sales as a unit of measurement will provide a basis for forecasting sales volume, and in turn, tax revenues. Similarly, a base study that converts employment forecasts into income forecasts makes possible a forecast of the yield of a local income tax.

A base study in a sense deals with the demand side of the economy, that is, where does it sell its products. In considering the future of the community it is also important to study the *supply side*. The supply side in effect deals with the nature of the local economy as an economic environment.[3] An obvious example of a necessary local supply condition is the case of a lumber town. No projection

---

[3] See the fine paper by Benjamin Chinitz, "Contrasts in Agglomeration: New York and Pittsburgh," *American Economic Review*, Proceedings LI (May, 1961) pp. 279-87.

of employment that will be created by future lumber exports makes sense if the area has just about exhausted its supply of timber. Some other qualifications to be noted on the supply side include: the existence of adequate financing for local enterprise, local enterpreneurs, a labor force with the skills to meet industry's needs, and available industrial sites.

Aspects of the supply side are highlighted by various types of studies such as industry studies, feasibility studies, and inventories of community assets and liabilities. *Industry studies* seek detailed information on the prospects for the area's major export industry, e.g., steel in Pittsburgh and tourism in Miami. *Feasibility studies,* or comparative cost studies as they are sometimes called, seek to determine the profitability to specific industries of locating within the community. Does this industry fit here? *Inventories of community assets and liabilities,* as the name implies, look more broadly at the assets for and liabilities against growth.

In short, any projection of long-run growth must pay attention to local supply factors. It would be erroneous to assume that every community is uniform with respect to these factors. Studies of local supply factors have an additional if perhaps more oblique influence. They direct attention to such matters as availability of sites and labor skills where community action can be especially fruitful in correcting deficiencies. If a community will honestly examine its local supply situation, significant improvements may be possible.[4]

---

[4] The term "honestly" is used in the hope that communities will avoid "huff and puff." Huff arises when community leaders merely assert that such things as high taxes or high wages are the cause of all their ills. Puff enters when brochures proclaim that the community's labor force is above average in skills and responsibility. (It is a never ending source of statistical surprise that all communities are above the national average.)

Chapter 3

How to Undertake
An Economic Base Study

Before starting the actual work of carrying out an economic base study, several decisions should be made so that the objectives, scope, and form of the study are clearly understood and so that the community will obtain the full use of the results. Many of these decisions will be made almost concurrently, such as determining who will sponsor the study and the area it will cover. For exposition purposes, however, this chapter presents these considerations separately.

Sponsorship

Nearly every community has some public or private group which has considered undertaking an economic base study. If the area has an official planning and development agency, this organization would be an appropriate sponsor since it can use the results in many ways and is concerned with the whole area. In the absence of an official agency, as in most metropolitan areas, a special council of local governments would be an appropriate sponsor. A nonprofit organization of community leaders would also be an appropriate group to undertake a base study. Which group initiates a base study is important because it will influence the area to be included, the level of financial support, and the degree to which local residents and firms cooperate.

Obtaining broad support helps to assure selection of a feasible area, financial support, and cooperation of local firms and residents in supplying information. Broad representation is also important because objective studies will usually reveal different rates of growth or decline among various sections and among various industries within the study area. The findings may imply unpleasant prospects for some sections and industries. Communities should objectively face the possibility of decline as well as growth and adjust their policies accordingly. A tendency to reject or discount a study because of distasteful findings may be at least partially neutralized if the study is initiated and conducted with broad community support.

Geographic Area to Include

No single geographic area is most appropriate for a base study. Many areas are appropriate, such as the labor supply area, the trading area, and the metropolitan area. Each has some merit. Yet, what is to be included is a matter of judgment.

Imagine that the possible geographic units are like concentric circles around some center. The center unit may be the city. The next larger may be the county, followed perhaps by the metropolitan area,[1] then the commuting area, and finally, the trading area. The point that is relevant is not the particular area chosen, but the effects of choosing alternative boundaries. If the city is the unit, exports will be high. A good deal of retail trade with suburbs will assure this result. As a larger unit is chosen, these sales will move out of the export and into the local category.

That there is no most appropriate area does not mean there are no standards for choosing a geographic unit. Many factors are helpful in making the choice. Governmental units are generally policy making bodies. The city naturally is the area of concern to city officials. It is not that they are uninterested in the larger units. They realize that what goes on in the metropolitan area as a whole will affect the city. But in terms of policy, only the city is their bailiwick. Thus, if a base study will be used as an aid in planning, estimating future service needs, determining tax levels, and other such governmental concerns, political boundaries are important. On the other hand, an area-wide Chamber of Commerce would be interested in the market potential of a larger area.

An economic base study is appropriate for practically any size area from a single suburban community on up. But a study of a single community within a larger economic area can be much more useful if a study is also available for the larger economic area of which it is a part because interpretation of information for the smaller area depends heavily upon knowledge of how it fits into the larger unit.

The metropolitan area is an appropriate one for an economic base study. Because the boundaries of metropolitan areas are determined largely by commuting and shopping patterns, this unit encompasses problems commonly referred to as "area-wide" or "metropolitan" in scope. A base study for a metropolitan area will also produce side payoffs for communities within the area. It will enable a community to see how it fits within the over-all structure of the area. For example, the growth of the suburban fringe depends in part upon the growth of the metropolitan region. A comprehensive base study at the metropolitan level can also generate data useful to particular communities. By way of example, an areawide survey of consumer incomes can produce income data not only for the metropolitan area, but, with the addition of a few questions, for sub-regions as well.

The economic base concept also applies to single suburban communities. The suburban community is part of an urban complex. Typically, it is commuter oriented with only a smattering of local industry other than retail trade and services. Smallness and proximity to an urban area mean that the economic interrelations within the suburb are small. But a base study is certainly appropriate for suburbs. For one thing, it is inexpensive to conduct. More important, unless preventative steps are taken, "urban blight" can become suburban blight. There is no excuse for the lack of economic information which exists in many suburban communities. The cost of economic information is trivial when compared to the ultimate cost of not having it.

Of course, for a suburb one fact will surely emerge: it is tied to the metropolitan area. A better understanding of the suburban community's future, as

---

[1] The term "metropolitan area" refers to the Standard Metropolitan Statistical Area (S.M.S.A.) as defined by the U. S. Department of Commerce.

noted above, requires an understanding of the general area economic forces.

Finally, differences in the availability of published data for various areas affects the choice of the area to study. If some larger unit such as a trading area is chosen, data must be gathered for smaller units and pieced together. Not every unit has uniform data and for comparability one must reduce the informational detail to that of the poorest unit.

The Cost of a Base Study

The cost of an economic base study can range from a few thousand dollars on up. There are so many variables that no set of estimates can account for the differences in the range of costs for various types of studies in different size areas.

The type of study will importantly influence the cost. A study using indirect measures of the economic base will cost less than one making direct measures. Studies which require original data that must be developed whether through mail questionnaires or personal interviews cost considerably more than those based on published data.

Community size will influence the cost. The larger the community the more the study is apt to cost.

A forecast included with the study will raise the cost considerably, depending upon the effort involved in making the forecast.

Other factors that will influence cost include the *availability of data,* the *degree of detail and accuracy desired,* and the *unit of measurement,* as discussed in Part II.

The large number of variable factors show why no cost schedule can be set forth that will apply to every community. Nevertheless, a broad range can be suggested.

Suppose a community where employment totaled 25,000 wanted to carry out a base study. If a study were based only on published data and indirect measures of the economic base, and no surveys were conducted, the cost would probably run in the $2,000 to $5,000 range.

For this same community, a study using available data plus a mail sample survey of firms, similar to the one carried out for Los Angeles described in Chapter 4 of Part II, would cost in the $8,000 to $15,000 range.

If both surveys of firms and personal interviews with a sample of 500 residents were involved, the cost could amount to $30,000 or more.

Making an associated forecast with any of the examples outlined would add to the cost.

It should be stressed that figures given above are only rough approximations of the costs involved, which is all that it is possible to give. It is suggested that groups embarking on an economic base study estimate the costs as carefully as possible to make sure that they have sufficient funds to complete the type of study they want and to distribute the findings widely.

Someone to Direct the Study

Who should actually carry out the study? This involves planning the study, collecting data, analyzing data, and preparing both technical and general reports.

Carrying out a worthwhile base study requires technical ability and training. Three sources for study direction can be suggested:

1. the staff of various local organizations,
2. consulting firms,
3. nearby university faculties.

If the study is not too large, someone on a local organization's staff trained in economics can direct the study. The staff of the local planning commission carried out the first economic base study of Metropolitan Dade County (Miami, Florida). If such staff people are not available and the study requires more expertise than is available locally, outside help is necessary.[2]

Consulting firms are one source of specialized help. As in any technical field, the problem is to select one competent in this field.

The economics faculty of a nearby university is another place to seek help. Many universities have faculty people qualified to direct a base study. Such persons are frequently interested in and knowledgeable about the community and would like to undertake such a study.

In many states the state department of commerce or economic development or the state planning board can help communities in selecting qualified consulting firms and economists. Other sources of assistance include the Area Redevelopment Administration of the U. S. Department of Commerce and the Urban Renewal Administration of the U. S. Housing and Home Finance Agency.

Local Cooperation in Supplying Data

The more relevant published data available, the easier the task of carrying out the study. Availability of data varies from community to community depending upon community size and how well the particular state and locality have compiled material. The sources of data are so varied that there is little sense in presenting a list. Discussion with persons who have worked on community economic problems and a brief survey of available sources will reveal the various types of published data.[3] This information is needed in designing a study and in estimating its cost.

Whoever carries out the study will need local cooperation above and beyond financial support. Obtaining data from local firms and residents requires the cooperation of the respondents. Broad support involving many local groups and a clear understanding of the reasons for and the benefits of a study will help obtain the necessary cooperation from those asked to supply information.

Wide Distribution of Results

There are a large number of potential readers and users of the information developed in an economic base study. The larger the number of persons who read

---

[2] Where outside help is required, it is extremely worthwhile to have the staff participate in the study. Their participation in the study provides them with necessary training so that the study can be repeated at intervals and changing patterns analyzed.

[3] A comprehensive list of Federal data sources is found in *Inventory of Federal Statistics for Standard Metropolitan Statistical Areas, Counties and Cities*, U. S. Bureau of the Budget (mimeographed) Washington, D. C., January, 1961.

it and use it, the more rewarding the study will be. Thus the findings should be distributed widely.

In addition to a non-technical report presenting the general results of an economic base study, the more detailed technical information developed should be made available. Technical reports might be published. Alternatively, the files of the detailed data gathered might be made available.

The typical citizen will not quickly digest all of the information developed by an economic base study. Yet some of the over-all magnitudes and implications can be presented so as to be useful to citizens in the formulation and execution of community decisions. For example, an economic base study can point up the importance to the community of small firms which provide basic employment. If these firms are to continue to operate profitably their problems must be recognized in community decisions.

Information developed in a base study can be especially fruitful in teaching economics to school children. One of the best ways to impart an understanding of economics is by referring to the local economy. This is a tangible and meaningful arena to students. Sponsors of community studies would do well to pass along to teachers for use in teaching economics the information developed in a local economic base study.

Concluding Remarks

The reader now knows in general what economic base studies are about and some of their benefits and uses. As will be pointed out in Part II, economic base studies can vary widely in accuracy and amount of detail. Even the most intensive studies with hundreds of thousand dollar budgets are subject to errors. In spite of this limitation, economic base studies are eminently worthwhile. Moreover, the cost is not exorbitant. But the cost of not doing economic base studies and other community economic studies can be very high. Communities now face new and in many ways more difficult problems than they did in the past. Solutions to these problems require the best local information that can be developed. An economic base study can provide an important part of the needed information.

Part 2

Economic Base Analysis

The four following chapters which constitute Part II are concerned with the theoretical foundations and empirical mechanics which underlie an economic base study. They are addressed primarily to the people involved in the making of a base study.

Chapter 4 shows how the local economy can be looked at in terms of industry and market groupings. Chapter 5 indicates how these industries and markets can be measured. Chapter 6 discusses the economic interrelations between the industries and markets by elaborating on the simple base concept given in Chapter 1. Chapter 7 takes up the methods of forecasting which can be used in conjunction with economic base studies.

Chapter 4

The Structure of the Local Economy

The sum and substance of what is sought in an economic base study is an understanding of the sources and levels of income and employment in a community. To gain this understanding it is easiest to start with the income flows in a small community whose economic relations are simple. After that, income flows in larger communities can be analyzed in terms of key economic groupings.

The Mechanics of Community Income and Employment

The simple mechanics of the community income stream are vividly illustrated by the boom and ghost towns of western frontiers. By looking at such a hypothetical town, Minetown, it is possible to: (1) understand the mechanics of the community income stream; and (2) begin to develop a framework of analysis. The discussions can be cast in terms of either income or employment, since both move in the same direction. (The difference between the two units will be taken up later.) Let's turn to these in the order mentioned.

Before the Minetown community existed the income stream is, naturally, zero — a dry riverbed. To get things moving, assume a copper vein is discovered. The economic origins of Minetown in the Old West emerge.

At first the trade patterns are simple. Ore is sold for export out of Minetown and the receipts used to import the tools of production and necessities of life. In terms of flows, ore flows out and mining equipment and consumer goods flow in. In dollar units, dollars are gained via ore exports and lost to purchase the necessary imports.

In due course the merchants arrive: the grocer, barber, saloon-keeper, and other such local service enterprises. The arrival of these merchants affects both the size and destination of the income flow. Before, the dollars flowed out of Minetown to merchants some distance away. Now, they go to local merchants. The income stream swells as more dollars change hands. The stream does not swell, however, by the total amount of the purchases now made locally. Many of the sales dollars taken in by the merchants, in turn, flow out to pay for the goods they sell. Nevertheless, the income stream has risen.

At this juncture, it is useful to point out a variation on the same theme. Suppose a mining supply firm locates in Minetown. Instead of purchasing needed equipment outside of Minetown, the mines now purchase some locally. What is the effect on the income stream? As before, the stream rises. But again, not by the full amount of the local purchases, since the supply firm itself must spend part of the dollars to import its merchandise.

More generally, income will remain unchanged until something comes along to disturb the equilibrium. The disturbances may take a variety of forms. The substitution examples of locally produced goods for those previously imported illustrate one kind of disturbance. An increased demand for copper, resulting in increased exports, will also generate a higher income level. Just how much new income is generated will be taken up later.

A Framework of Analysis

The Minetown example points up some of the key economic groupings within a community. These groupings provide a useful framework to help understand the economic interrelations within communities. The rest of this chapter seeks to identify various groupings in such a manner that they can be fitted within a framework of analysis.

Sectors and Industries: Dividing up the Local Economy

Up to this point economic units have been placed either into the bin labeled "exports" or the "local" bin. But why limit to two bins? Why not have five, or ten or fifty? This raises the issue of the most useful level of aggregation. Except in extremely small communities, it is simply not feasible to consider the details of each and every economic unit. And yet, the loss of detail can hurt. Thus, a compromise between the value of detailed information and the costs of such information has to be evaluated in planning a study.

Aggregation can be of two kinds, "industry" and "sectors." Industries refer to aggregates of firms producing similar products. Sectors refer to the kinds of markets that industries serve.

Sectors: Sources of Demand

The division of the markets served by the local economy into two broad groups, export and local, provides an initial breakdown. These two distinct sources of demand can be called the export sector and the local sector. Each of these broad sectors can be broken down further into component sectors.

The selection of these component sectors depends upon the different types of demand for the community's products and the purpose and size of the study. Exports offer a good illustration of the issues involved in choosing sectors.

Exports stand apart from other sectors since their level is set by non-local market forces. Whether the exports are tobacco products from Durham, the flour products of the Twin Cities, or the tourists in Miami, all have their level set, by and large, by market forces outside the community.

Suppose Seattle, the home of Boeing Aircraft, is under study. Boeing sells a number of its commercial jets to national and international firms. Yet, Boeing is also part of the defense effort and deals with the Federal government. While these defense products are also exported, they serve a different kind of market, a market whose level is set more by political decisions in response to various defense needs. Exports to the Federal government, then, are one group which might well be identified as a separate sector. Hence, exports can be divided into private exports and government exports.[1]

There is, of course, no need to stop here. In some communities, it may be desirable to separate exports which go to foreign nations from those going to U. S. markets. This might be desirable since foreign markets are subject to different kinds of forces; e.g., import controls. The main point is that the sectors which can be usefully identified depend upon the particulars of each community and the characteristics of its market.

Exports were used as an illustration largely because they are more obvious. Yet, local sources of demand are not a homogeneous set. They, too, can be usefully sectored into subsets. A few possibilities will be suggested here. The next chapter will consider them in more detail.

Decisions by local business to invest in plant and equipment are often considered as subject to special economic forces; e.g., interest rates. Hence, it is useful to establish a separate sector, Business Investment. And, like business decisions, consumers' decisions to purchase dwelling units are also subject to different forces. Housing Investment, therefore, may also be usefully identified.

Of course, local consumer spending is one of the most important local

---

[1] It should be recognized that some private exports may end up imbedded in government products. For example, Philadelphia steel may be sold to a Connecticut aircraft engine firm which, in turn, sells to the Federal government. In terms of the Philadelphia economy, however, these sales are private exports. There are methods to account for this kind of an ultimate relationship to the Federal government, but they need not concern us here.

sectors. Most often base studies treat this as one sector, called Local Consumption. However, it can be broken down into subsectors, such as retail trade, services, and so forth, or durable and non-durable purchases. The degree and kind of detail depends on the intended use of the study.

Finally, for many of the reasons that the Federal government was treated as a separate sector, state and local government activities might also be considered a separate sector.

Just as with exports, there is no magic number of local sectors. These vary with community size, the purposes of the study, and similar factors. In Sioux City, Professor Leven considered two local sectors, investment and consumption.[2] Dr. Barbara Berman's model for projecting levels of activity for the New York Metropolitan Region added local government purchases as a sector.[3] In studies of San Francisco and Los Angeles, Professors W. Lee Hansen, R. Thayne Robson, and this writer created five local sectors: consumption, housing investment, business investment, state and local government current operation, and state and local government investments.[4]

Ties to Sectors: Direct and Indirect

The decision to delineate an export sector means that exports must be identified. This implies specifying both the direct ties and the indirect ties to export markets.

An example can highlight the differences between direct and indirect ties. In San Diego, California, a number of firms pack tuna fish for distribution to national markets. From the point of view of the San Diego economy, the employment and income is derived from exports. As one of the inputs used in the process of packing the tuna, tin cans are required. Some of these cans are purchased from local manufacturers. These are local sales of tin cans. Yet, should they be classified as local sales? Do they belong in the same group as barbershops, supermarkets, TV repair shops, and other activities serving the local market? Suppose, for a moment, that San Diego tuna packers owned their own tin can plants; i.e., they are more vertically integrated firms. Now, tin can employment would be classed as export. But this result is merely a result of the organization of particular firms. Capriciousness can be avoided if tin can production is placed in the export-linked category and classified as indirect exports. Tin cans are linked to exports inasmuch as a change in the export demand for tuna will change the demand for tin cans.

What about the sheet-metal supplier to the tin can firm? Why not include him in the export-linked category? Yet, if he is included, where does one stop? The stopping point can be visualized by supposing that tuna exports increase by, say, one million dollars a year. Keep all other things constant and assume, for now, that all of the supplying firms have excess capacity. (The assumption of excess capacity avoids bottleneck problems, e.g., a shortage of sheet-metal.) The

<hr />

[2]*Economic Report, 1959,* City Planning Commission, Sioux City, Iowa.

[3]Barbara Berman, Benjamin Chinitz, and Edgar Hoover, *Projection of a Metropolis,* Cambridge: Harvard University Press, 1960.

[4]W. Lee Hansen, R. Thayne Robson, and Charles M. Tiebout, *Markets for California Products,* California Economic Development Agency, Sacramento, California, 1961.

increase in direct exports is one million dollars. But additional sales will also arise — tin cans, sheet-metal, electric power, and all of the inputs needed to produce the extra canned tuna. Not only will the suppliers of inputs to the tuna packers increase their output, but so will the suppliers' suppliers, and so on down the line until the increased output is negligible. When all of the sales are added up, the total will be larger than one million. For not only are the export sales counted, but the sales of supplies to the exporter and so on through related industries. Thus, total transactions or turnover may amount to $2.5 million. The additional $1.5 above the one million of direct export sales represents the sales *indirectly* tied to exports.[5]

While the discussion has focused on exports, *the same general principles apply to other sectors* such as local consumer purchases and local business investment. A local brick manufacturer may be indirectly tied to local business investment. A local farmer who sells his output to a local ice cream manufacturer is indirectly tied to local consumers. Other examples are plentiful.

Industry Groupings

Just as the various demands faced by firms have been aggregated into sectors, so, too, can individual firms be aggregated into industries. This kind of aggregation is more familiar and can be disposed of with ease.

Industry aggregates usually follow the classification scheme set out in the *Standard Industrial Classification Manual*. The shorthand reference is to the "S.I.C. code." While the reference may not be familiar, the code is commonplace. Table I shows employment by the broadest industry group categories for Albuquerque, New Mexico.

Table 1

Employment by Industry Groups
Albuquerque, New Mexico, S.M.S.A., 1957

Industry Group	Employment	
Total		71,100
Agriculture	1,600	
Mining	200	
Contract Construction	4,700	
Manufacturing	10,200	
Transportation and Public Utilities	5,600	
Trade	15,700	
Finance	3,400	
Services	7,600	
Government	22,100	

Source: *Albuquerque Economic Supports Analysis,* General Plan Monograph 1, City Planning Department, April, 1958.

Often it is desirable to show finer industry detail. In the S.I.C. code, the broad industry groups are broken into more detailed industry groups. Manufac-

---

[5] There is an additional effect which may occur to the reader. As a result of the new direct and indirect sales local incomes will increase. Part of this will be spent locally on such items as, retail goods, housing, and services. This effect is treated separately in Chapter 6.

turing, for example, is made up of various sub-groups: food and kindred products, leather goods, transportation equipment, and so on. These sub-groups themselves have sub-groups. In the S.I.C. terminology, the broad groups, such as manufacturing, are identified by one digit. The next lower level is the two-digit group, e.g., S.I.C. 37 Transportation Equipment. This process goes on through three and down to four digits, e.g., S.I.C. 372 Aircraft and Parts and 3723 Aircraft Propellers and Parts.

The most useful level of aggregation depends upon the nature of the local economy. Table 2 illustrates the point. For Sioux City, Iowa, Professor Leven went into fine detail (three-digit, S.I.C.) for some industries and used the broad groups for other industries. A look at the industry descriptions, even without any regard to the numerical values, shows that food processing in general, and meat packing in particular, are important in Sioux City — as the employment data indicate.

Table 2
Employment by Industry Groups
Sioux City, Iowa, 1958

Description of Industry	S. I. C. Code No.	Employees Number	% of Total
Agriculture	01-07	115	0.4
Construction	15-17	819	2.5
Meat Packing	201	2,983	9.3
Other Food Processing	202-209	1,818	5.6
Other Manufacturing	23-39	3,572	11.1
Transportation & Utilities	40-49	2,751	8.5
Wholesale Trade	501-509	2,572	8.0
Retail Trade	52-59	6,914	21.5
Finance & Real Estate	60-67	1,432	4.4
Services	70-89	4,900	15.2
Government	91-93	4,329	13.5
Totals	01-93	32,205	100.0

Source: *Economic Report, 1959,* City Planning Commission, Sioux City, Iowa.

In most communities, the level of industry aggregation desired can be readily determined. Moreover, only rarely is there an excess of data by detailed industry groups. Usually, less data exist than one would like.

Sectors and Industries Combined

A better feeling for the questions involved in choosing both sectors and industry aggregates can be gained by looking at some data developed in connection with the Los Angeles study mentioned above.[6]

Table 3 shows a highly aggregative set of data. The employment created by the sales of all industries, in terms of per cent, are assigned either to the export or local sector. Table 4, with more rows, adds more industry detail. Just as the rows have been added to show more industry detail, so, too, with the columns expanded, more sector detail is given as shown in Table 5. Here, exports have been divided into two sectors: Private and to the Federal government. In addition, sales to local consumers (people) have also been identified. Other sectors can, and will, be added.

---

[6] Hansen, Robson, and Tiebout, *op. cit.*

Table 3
Allocation of Employment Created by Sales of all Industries
Los Angeles-Long Beach, California, S.M.S.A., 1960

Industry From	Sector To	Employment (In thousands)			Distribution of Employment	
		Total	Export	Local	Export	Local
All Industries		2,649.0	715.2	1,933.8	27.0%	73.0%

Source: Hansen, Robson, and Tiebout, *Markets for California Products*, California Economic Development Agency, Sacramento, 1961.

Table 4
Allocation of Employment Created by Sales of Industry Groups
Los Angeles-Long Beach, California, S.M.S.A., 1960

Industry From	Sector To	Employment (In thousands)			Distribution of Employment	
		Total	Export	Local	Export	Local
Durable Manufacturers		579.7	381.5	198.2	65.6%	34.4%
Primary Metals		26.2	9.5	16.7	36.1	63.9
Fabricated Metals		65.2	27.9	37.3	42.6	57.4
Non-Electrical Machinery		61.0	45.9	15.1	75.0	25.0
Electrical Machinery		113.0	82.4	30.6	72.9	27.1
Transportation Equipment		200.7	143.5	57.2	71.7	28.3
Instruments & Ordnance		41.4	34.6	6.8	86.3	16.4
Stone, Clay & Glass		22.0	15.4	6.6	70.0	30.0
Lumber Products		8.4	2.5	5.9	29.7	70.3
Furniture Products		26.0	11.9	14.1	45.7	54.3
Miscellaneous Manufacturers		15.8	7.9	7.9	50.1	49.0
Non-Durable Manufacturers		233.4	104.6	128.8	44.8	55.2
Apparel		48.2	34.7	13.5	72.0	28.0
Textile-Leather		9.5	4.7	4.8	49.5	50.5
Paper		13.7	9.4	4.3	68.8	31.2
Printing		38.4	9.3	29.1	24.1	75.9
Chemicals		23.3	12.9	10.4	55.4	44.6
Petroleum		18.8	6.8	12.0	36.2	63.8
Rubber		23.7	13.6	10.1	57.4	42.6
Food & Beverages		57.8	13.2	44.6	22.9	77.1
Total Manufacturing		813.1	486.1	327.0	59.7	40.3
Agriculture, Forestry, Fisheries & Mining		47.3	5.3	42.0	11.2	88.2
Contract Construction		163.9	.5	163.4	.3	99.7
Transportation, Communication & Public Utilities		147.6	52.4	95.2	35.5	64.5
Wholesale Trade		161.7	24.2	137.5	15.0	85.0
Retail Trade		429.9	40.2	389.7	9.4	90.6
Finance, Ins. & Real Estate		131.5	22.1	109.4	16.8	83.2
Services		476.2	63.2	413.0	13.3	86.7
Government		277.8	21.2	256.6	7.6	92.4
Total All Industries		**2,649.0**	**715.2**	**1,933.8**	**27.0**	**73.0**

Note: The percentages after the decimal point were included to avoid gross errors in rounding.
Source: Same as Table 3.

Table 5
Allocation of Employment Created by Sales of Industry Groups;
Exports Private, Exports Government, Local Consumption, and All Other Sales
Los Angeles-Long Beach, California, S.M.S.A., 1960
(In per cents)

Industry From \ Sector To	Exports Private	Exports Fed. Govt.	Local Consumption	All Other Sales
Durable Manufacturers	30.5	35.3	.7	33.5
Primary Metals	26.6	9.5	1.9	62.0
Fabricated Metals	27.6	15.0	1.1	56.3
Non-Electrical Machinery	66.5	8.5	—	25.0
Electrical Machinery	26.1	46.8	.2	26.9
Transportation Equipment	17.4	54.3	.1	28.2
Instruments & Ordnance	26.3	57.3	.5	15.9
Stone, Clay & Glass	68.6	1.4	2.7	27.3
Lumber Products	15.4	14.3	—	70.3
Furniture	44.5	1.2	6.9	47.4
Misc. Manufacturers	50.1	—	.6	49.3
Non-Durable Manufacturers	41.7	3.1	10.9	44.3
Apparel	69.1	2.9	—	28.0
Textile-Leather	47.4	2.1	1.1	49.4
Paper	68.8	—	.7	30.5
Printing	24.1	—	6.8	69.1
Chemicals	52.0	3.4	25.3	19.3
Petroleum	29.3	6.9	—	63.8
Rubber	46.0	11.4	.4	42.2
Foods & Beverages	21.5	1.4	28.9	48.2
Total Manufacturing	33.7	26.0	3.7	36.6
Agriculture, Forestry, Fisheries & Mining	7.8	3.4	—	88.8
Contract Construction	—	.3	—	99.7
Transpn., Comm. & Pub. Util.	33.2	2.3	27.8	36.7
Wholesale Trade	14.5	.5	.7	84.3
Retail Trade	9.4	—	82.6	7.9
Finance, Ins. & Real Estate	16.1	.7	38.3	44.9
Services	12.6	.7	67.3	19.4
Government	—	7.6	—	92.4
Total All Industries	17.8	9.2	30.1	42.9

Source: Same as Table 3.

Before doing this, however, it is important to recognize that industries in Los Angeles may sell their products and services not only to sectors but also to "Local Industries" in the area. For example, a local bakery may export part of its products (the Exports-Private Sector), deliver some directly to local consumers (the Local Consumption Sector), and sell the rest to Local Industries. (In this case, the Local Industries are likely to be retail stores and restaurants.) Thus, 100 per cent of the bakery's sales have been accounted for.

Table 6 introduces the additional sectors: Business Investment, Housing Investment, State and Local Government Current Operations, and State and Local Government Investments. Also added is a column for sales to Local Industries (Column 8). Note, for example, that the industry, Primary Metals, (Row 2) sold 53.8 per cent of its output in 1960 to Local Industries (Column 8) in the Los Angeles area. The rest, 46.2 per cent, was sold to the sectors as listed in the first seven column headings.

The full meaning of this new type of column (Column 8) is more readily grasped by indicating how the estimate was derived. Firms in the Primary Metals Industry were asked what percentage of their sales went to each of the seven

34

Table 6
Allocation of Employment Created by
Sales of Industry Groups to Seven Sectors and Local Industries
Los Angeles-Long Beach, California, S.M.S.A., 1960
(In Per cents)

Sectors & Local Ind. To / Industry From	1 Exports Private	2 Exports Govt.	3 Local Cons.	4 Invest. - Bus	5 Invest. - Hsg.	6 Govt. Current	7 Govt. Inv.	8 Local Inds.
1 Durable Mfrs.	30.5	35.3	.7	5.9	—	.2	.4	27.0
2 Primary Mtls.	26.6	9.5	1.9	6.5	—	.4	1.1	53.8
3 Fab. Metals	27.6	15.0	1.1	.5	—	.6	.3	54.8
4 Non-Elec. Mchy.	66.5	8.5	—	17.9	—	—	.7	6.2
5 Elec. Mchy.	26.1	46.8	.2	12.6	—	—	.4	13.9
6 Transpn. Equip.	17.4	54.3	.1	2.4	—	—	—	25.9
7 Instr. & Ord.	26.3	57.3	.5	.5	—	.2	.2	15.0
8 Stone, Clay, Glass	68.6	1.4	2.7	—	—	.9	—	26.4
9 Lumber Products	15.4	14.3	—	—	—	—	—	70.3
10 Furn. & Fixtures	44.5	1.2	6.9	8.1	—	.8	1.9	36.5
11 Misc. Mfrs.	50.1	—	.6	—	—	—	—	49.4
12 Non-Durable Mfrs.	41.7	3.1	10.9	.6	—	.3	—	43.4
13 Apparel	69.1	2.9	—	—	—	—	—	28.0
14 Textile-Leather	47.4	2.1	1.1	—	—	—	—	49.5
15 Paper	68.8	—	.7	.7	—	.7	—	29.2
16 Printing	24.1	—	6.8	—	—	.3	—	68.8
17 Chemicals	62.0	3.4	25.3	—	—	.9	—	18.5
18 Petroleum	29.3	6.9	—	—	—	—	—	63.8
19 Rubber	46.0	11.4	.4	5.5	—	—	—	36.7
20 Foods & Bevgs.	21.5	1.4	28.9	—	—	.2	—	47.9
21 Total Mfrg.	33.7	26.0	3.7	4.4	—	.2	.3	31.7
22 Agric., Forestry, Fisheries, Mining	7.8	3.4	—	—	—	—	—	88.8
23 Contract Constrn.	—	.3	—	31.1	49.6	—	19.0	—
24 Transpn., Comm. Public Utilities	33.2	2.3	27.8	—	—	3.0	—	33.7
25 Wholesale Trade	14.5	.5	.7	—	—	.1	—	84.2
26 Retail Trade	9.4	—	82.6	.1	—	.9	—	6.9
27 Finance, Insur., Real Estate	16.1	.7	38.3	4.5	20.1	—	.5	19.8
28 Services	12.6	.7	67.3	.9	2.8	1.0	.1	14.8
29 Government	—	7.6	—	—	—	91.1	1.3	—
30 Total All Industries	17.8	9.2	30.1	3.7	4.6	10.1	1.4	23.0

Note: Blank entries indicate sales are either zero or negligible
Source: Same as Table 3.

sectors shown. Where were the other sales made? The answer has to be to other local industries. Hence, the entries for Column 8.

The next question to ask is: What "Local Industries" bought these products? Returning to the example of Primary Metals products, Table 7 indicates in percentages of total sales the local industries to which Primary Metals output were sold. Note that some 23.7 per cent of the sales went to the local Fabricated Metals industry (Column 16). Since Primary Metals includes steel foundries, rolling mills, and similar industries, it is not surprising that a relatively large proportion, 23.7 per cent, is sold to fabricators for further processing.

A complete table for Los Angeles similar to the Primary Metals table is shown as Table 8. (Some of the particular entries, which may be a bit puzzling,

Table 7

Allocation of Employment Created by Sales of
Primary Metals Industry to Sectors and Local Industry Groups
Los Angeles-Long Beach, California, S.M.S.A., 1960
(In Per cents)

Sector or Ind. To — Industry From	1 Exp. Pri.	2 Exp. Gov.	3 Loc. Con.	4 Inv. Bus.	5 Inv. Hsg.	6 Gov. Cur.	7 Gov. Inv.	8 Loc. Ind.	9 Agr. Etc.	10 Con. Cnstn.	11 Trnsp. Etc.	12 Ret. Trade	13 Fin. Ins.	14 Ser-vices	15 Pri. Mtls.	16 Fab. Mtls. (con't.)
Primary Metals	26.6	9.5	1.9	6.5	—	.4	1.1	53.8	—	2.7	—	.8	—	—	1.9	23.7

	17 Non-El Mchy.	18 El. Mchy.	19 Trnsp. Equip.	20 Inst. Ord.	21 Stone Etc.	22 Lbr. Prod.	23 Furn.	24 Misc. Mfrs.	25 Ap-parel	26 Tex-tile	27 Paper	28 Print-ing	29 Chem.	30 Petro-leum	31 Rub-ber	32 Foods, Bevs.	33 Total Sales
Primary Metals (con't.)	9.9	2.7	5.0	1.5	—	—	3.1	—	—	—	.4	—	—	2.3	—	—	100.0%

Source: Same as Table 3.

reflect certain definitions used in the study. These particulars need not be considered.) If this sort of table seems far removed from more familiar economic base tables, the difference is merely one of detail or level of aggregation, as will be shown in a moment.

The next step in the analysis may seem to involve some sleight of hand, but those familiar with the iterative (tracing through) process will recognize immediately how the next table was derived. Both Tables 7 and 8 show that 23.7 per cent of the sales of Primary Metals output went as inputs to the Fabricated Metals industry (Row 2, Column 16). What did the Fabricated Metals industry do with these inputs? They further processed these inputs and sold them to their customers, just as in the earlier example the San Diego tuna packers took the tin cans as inputs and incorporated them in their product. But where does the, Fabricated Metals industry sell its products? Row 3 of Table 8 gives the answer. For example, 15.0 per cent of Fabricated Metals sales are to the Federal government (Row 3, Column 2). Thus, the Primary Metals industry is linked or indirectly tied to the Federal government. In fact, through Fabricated Metals alone they are tied by the amount, 23.7% x 15.0% equals 3.6% of Primary Metals sales.

The Fabricated Metals industry has other customers as Row 3 indicates. One of these is the Transportation Equipment industry (Column 19) to whom it sells 4.2 per cent of its output. But to whom does the Transportation Equipment industry sell? Row 6 gives the answer. Note that 54.3 per cent goes to the Federal government, mostly aircraft and space vehicles. Thus, the Primary Metals industry is indirectly tied, through the Fabricated Metals industry and on through the Transportation Equipment industry to the Federal government. The appropriate per cent is 23.7% x 4.2% x 54.3% equals .54% of Primary Metals sales.

If this process is carried out step by step, over and over again, eventually all sales originally to Local Industries will end up as indirect sales to one of the seven sectors. In economic base jargon, the linked industries will have been traced out. Table 9 shows the results of such a process. For each industry, the percentage of total sales directly to a sector are shown in the first row. The second row indicates the percentage of total sales indirectly tied to a sector. The third row is the sum of the first two rows.

Now what comes out of all this? Table 9, which traces out direct and indirect ties, presents an economic base study of Los Angeles. A look at the last entry, Total Sales (Row 30), indicates the over-all picture. If all export industries are considered basic and all others non-basic, then in terms of the unit sales, 36 per cent is basic (Columns 1 and 2) and 64 per cent is non-basic (Columns 3-7). The basic/non-basic ratio is 36/64.[7] Seen in this light, Los Angeles has been divided up just as Minetown. The difference is one of degree in sectoring and in tracing out industry interrelations.

---

[7] The reader may notice that the per cent of total employment assigned to exports has jumped from 27 per cent in Table 3 to 36 per cent in Table 9. This is so because indirect exports have been taken into account.

37

Table 8

Allocation of Employment Created by Sales of Industry Groups to Sectors and Local Industry Groups

Los Angeles-Long Beach, California, S.M.S.A., 1960

Demand Sectors & Industry To / Industry From	1 Exports — Private	2 Exports — Government	3 Local Consumption	4 Investment — Business	5 Investment — Housing	6 Govt. — Current	7 Govt. — Investment	8 Local Industries	9 Agric., For., Fish., Min.	10 Contract Constrcn.	11 Trnspn., Comm., P.U.	12 Retail Trade	13 Finance, Ins. & R. E.	14 Services
1 Durable Mfrs.	30.5	35.3	.7	5.9	—	.2	.4	27.0	.5	1.9	.8	5.2	—	.2
2 Primary Metals	26.6	9.5	1.9	6.5	—	.4	1.1	53.8	—	2.7	—	.8	—	—
3 Fabricated Metals	27.6	15.0	1.1	.5	—	.6	.3	54.8	—	7.7	.8	6.6	.2	.2
4 Non-Elec. Machy.	66.5	8.5	—	17.9	—	—	.7	6.2	.2	.8	.5	.3	—	.2
5 Electrical Machy.	26.1	46.8	.2	12.6	—	—	.4	13.9	—	.4	.1	3.2	—	—
6 Transprtn. Equip.	17.4	54.3	.1	2.4	—	—	—	25.9	—	—	1.8	5.2	—	.5
7 Instruments & Ord.	26.3	57.3	.5	.5	—	.2	.2	15.0	—	—	.5	.2	—	—
8 Stone, Clay, Glass	68.6	1.4	2.7	—	—	.9	—	26.4	1.8	9.5	—	8.6	—	—
9 Lumber Products	15.4	14.3	—	—	—	—	—	70.3	29.7	10.7	—	2.4	—	—
10 Furn. & Fixtures	44.5	1.2	6.9	8.1	—	.8	1.9	36.5	—	1.9	.8	30.8	—	.4
11 Misc. Mfrs.	50.1	—	.6	—	—	—	—	49.4	.6	3.8	—	8.2	—	—
12 Non-Durable Mfrs.	41.7	3.1	10.9	.6	—	.3	—	43.4	1.2	1.5	3.5	24.8	.6	.8
13 Apparel	69.1	2.9	—	—	—	—	—	28.0	.6	—	—	26.6	—	—
14 Textile-Leather	47.4	2.1	1.1	—	—	—	—	49.5	1.1	—	—	48.3	—	—
15 Paper	68.8	—	.7	.7	—	.7	—	29.2	—	—	.7	14.0	.7	—
16 Printing	24.1	—	6.8	—	—	.3	—	68.8	.3	2.3	12.0	27.0	3.1	2.9
17 Chemicals	52.0	3.4	25.3	—	—	.9	—	18.5	—	3.0	1.7	6.1	—	.4
18 Petroleum	29.3	6.9	—	—	—	—	—	63.8	—	1.6	16.0	28.2	—	3.7
19 Rubber	46.0	11.4	.4	5.5	—	—	—	36.7	2.1	7.2	—	3.0	—	—
20 Foods & Beverages	21.5	1.4	28.9	—	—	.2	—	47.9	3.3	—	—	36.0	—	—
21 Total Manufactrg.	33.7	26.0	3.7	4.4	—	.2	.3	31.7	.1	1.8	1.6	10.8	.2	.4
22 Agriculture. Etc.	7.8	3.4	—	—	—	—	—	88.8	3.8	—	—	25.6	—	—
23 Contract Constrcn.	—	.3	—	31.1	49.6	—	19.0	—	—	—	—	—	—	—
24 Trnspn., Comm., Etc.	33.2	2.3	27.8	—	—	3.0	—	33.7	.3	2.1	1.0	9.6	.9	3.3
25 Wholesale Trade	14.5	.5	.7	—	—	.1	—	84.2	.1	11.1	.4	51.0	.4	1.8
26 Retail Trade	9.4	—	82.6	.1	—	.9	—	6.9	.1	3.1	.1	—	.3	.8
27 Fin., Ins., Re. Est.	16.1	.7	38.3	4.5	20.1	—	.5	19.8	.2	1.4	1.5	4.8	1.1	3.5
28 Services	12.6	.7	67.3	.9	2.8	1.0	.1	14.8	.1	.3	.7	4.7	1.3	2.5
29 Government	—	7.6	—	—	—	91.1	1.3	—	—	—	—	—	—	—
30 Total Sales	17.8	9.2	30.1	3.7	4.6	10.1	1.4	23.0	.4	2.0	.8	8.5	.5	1.2

Source: Same as Table 3.

Table 8   (continued)

15 Primary Metals	16 Fabricated Metals	17 Non-Elec. Machinery	18 Electrical Machinery	19 Transprtn. Equipment	20 Instrumnts. & Ordnance	21 Stone, Clay & Glass	22 Lumber Products	23 Furniture	24 Misc. Manufs.	25 Apparel	26 Textile-Leather	27 Paper	28 Printing	29 Chemicals	30 Petroleum	31 Rubber	32 Foods & Beverages	33 Total Sales
.2	5.0	1.1	1.2	5.8	2.6	.2	.1	.3	.5	—	—	.1	.1	1.0	.2	.1	.1	100.0
1.9	23.7	9.9	2.7	5.0	1.5	—	—	3.1	—	—	—	.4	—	—	2.3	—	—	100.0
.5	24.2	.2	.5	4.2	3.5	.5	.5	.9	2.5	—	—	.3	—	.9	.2	.2	.3	100.0
—	1.0	.5	.7	1.0	.5	—	—	—	—	—	—	—	.7	—	—	—	—	100.0
—	—	—	3.6	4.6	2.0	—	—	—	—	—	—	—	—	—	—	—	—	100.0
—	3.2	1.5	—	9.0	4.5	—	—	—	.1	—	—	—	—	—	—	—	—	100.0
—	—	—	2.7	11.4	.2	—	—	—	—	—	—	—	—	—	—	—	—	100.0
.5	—	—	—	—	—	2.3	—	—	—	—	—	—	—	.9	—	.5	2.3	100.0
1.2	1.2	1.2	1.2	4.8	7.1	1.2	2.4	—	1.2	—	—	—	—	2.4	2.4	1.2	—	100.0
—	—	—	—	1.2	—	—	—	1.5	—	—	—	—	—	—	—	—	—	100.0
—	—	—	—	—	—	—	—	—	5.1	—	—	—	—	31.6	—	—	—	100.0
.5	.6	.3	.1	.7	.5	—	—	.3	.3	—	—	—	2.7	1.4	.3	1.4	1.8	100.0
—	—	—	—	.8	—	—	—	—	—	—	—	—	—	—	—	—	—	100.0
—	—	—	—	—	—	—	—	—	—	—	—	—	—	—	—	—	—	100.0
—	—	—	.7	.7	—	—	—	.7	—	—	—	—	—	.7	—	—	10.5	100.0
.8	—	.3	.3	.3	.3	.3	—	—	.5	—	.3	—	16.3	1.0	—	.3	—	100.0
.4	.4	—	—	1.3	.4	—	—	—	—	—	—	—	—	1.3	2.6	.4	.4	100.0
3.7	3.7	3.2	—	—	—	—	—	—	—	—	—	—	—	—	—	3.7	—	100.0
—	2.1	—	—	3.4	4.2	—	—	2.5	1.7	—	—	—	—	—	.4	10.1	—	100.0
—	—	—	—	—	—	—	—	—	—	—	—	—	—	4.2	—	—	4.5	100.0
.3	3.8	.8	.8	4.3	2.0	.1	.1	.3	.4	—	—	—	.8	1.1	.2	.4	.6	100.0
—	—	—	—	—	—	5.3	—	—	—	—	—	—	—	2.1	21.4	—	30.6	100.0
—	—	—	—	—	—	—	—	—	—	—	—	—	—	—	—	—	—	100.0
.6	1.3	1.2	2.3	4.2	.8	.5	.1	.5	.3	.9	.1	.3	.7	.5	.4	.5	1.2	100.0
.6	1.5	1.4	2.7	4.9	1.0	.5	.2	.6	.4	1.1	.2	.3	.9	.6	.4	.6	1.4	100.0
.1	.2	.2	.3	.7	.1	.1	—	.1	.1	.1	.1	.1	.1	.1	.1	.1	.2	100.0
.2	.6	.5	.9	1.7	.3	.2	.1	.2	.2	.5	.2	.2	.4	.2	.2	.2	.5	100.0
.2	.4	.4	.7	1.3	.3	.1	—	.2	.1	.3	—	.1	.3	.1	.1	.1	.4	100.0
—	—	—	—	—	—	—	—	—	—	—	—	—	—	—	—	—	—	100.0
.2	1.5	.5	.8	2.3	.8	.2	.1	.2	.2	.2	.1	.1	.4	.5	.5	.2	1.0	100.0

Defining the Sectors

Now that the concept of direct and indirect ties to various sectors is understood, it is necessary to define for empirical purposes these sectors and whether a tie is direct or indirect. Two examples of the kinds of questions to be resolved with respect to sectors are: Is tourist spending export income? Is the employment associated with construction of a new apartment building assigned to housing investment or business investment? With respect to direct versus indirect ties, questions might be asked such as: Is a lumber dealer tied directly to housing investment or only indirectly through the contractor? Are subcontractors tied directly to the Federal government or only indirectly through the prime contractor? The following discussion considers these issues with respect to the various sectors.

Exports — Private

Private exports constitute the receipt from transactions with the sales to non-residents, excluding the Federal government. The main items are the goods and services which flow outside the community's borders. Also included are local purchases by non-residents — the importance of tourists to some areas is an example. Items which are less obvious, such as dividend income, private pension receipts, and rental income from non-local property also constitute part of the export private sector. The rule of thumb in classifying exports is whether or not the community receives dollars from private outside sources. To many, the criteria for exports will strike a familiar note. Essentially, the community is looked at as a small nation. The items which enter as exports for a nation also apply to a community.

For the export sector the difference between employment and income as units of measure can be of some importance. Employment measures the direct and indirect jobs associated with exports. But suppose, for example, a community's exports consisted entirely of retired persons living on pensions paid from outside sources. No export employment exists, yet the local sectors will show employment. Differences of this sort should be recognized.

Exports — Government

Exports to the Federal government need not be defined as actually leaving the community. Sales to a local military base may not cross the community's boundaries. However, these sales differ from other local sales; the volume depends upon Federal actions. Thus, it is useful to consider exports to the Federal government really as sales to the Federal government.

If sales to the Federal government is adopted as the appropriate definition of this sector, two minor points should be noted. First, civilian employees of the Federal government and their income constitute part of this sector. Just as a corner grocer is assigned to the local consumption sector, civilian Federal employees would be assigned to exports to the Federal government. In like manner, military personnel can be treated as exports to the Federal government. (This presumes, of course, that military personnel are considered as residents of the community, not as non-residents such as tourists.)

Just as in the case of private exports, firms can be tied indirectly to the

Table 9
Allocation of Employment Created by
Sales of Industry Groups to Sectors, Direct and Indirect
Los Angeles-Long Beach, California, S.M.S.A., 1960
(In per cents)

Demand Sec. & Ind. To: Industry Group From	1 Exports Private	2 Exports Govt.	3 Local Cons.	4 Invest. - Bus.	5 Invest. - Hsg.	6 Govt. Current	7 Govt. - Inv.	Total
1 Durable Mfrs.								
Direct	31.0	35.3	5.1	5.9	—	.2	.4	77.9
Indirect	7.2	8.5	2.7	1.6	1.4	.1	.6	22.1
Total	38.2	43.8	7.8	7.5	1.4	.3	1.0	100.0
2 Primary Mtls.								
Direct	26.7	9.5	2.7	6.5	—	.4	1.1	46.9
Indirect	23.3	14.9	5.3	5.0	2.7	.4	1.5	53.1
Total	50.0	24.4	8.0	11.5	2.7	.8	2.6	100.0
3 Fab. Metals								
Direct	28.2	15.2	6.6	.5	—	.6	.3	51.4
Indirect	16.9	13.8	5.5	4.1	5.5	.3	2.5	48.6
Total	45.1	29.0	12.1	4.6	5.5	.9	2.8	100.0
12 Non-Durable Mfrs.								
Direct	44.1	3.1	31.5	.6	—	.4	—	79.7
Indirect	7.4	2.3	6.8	1.3	1.6	.3	.6	20.3
Total	51.5	5.4	38.3	1.9	1.6	.7	.6	100.0
13 Apparel								
Direct	71.6	2.9	22.0	—	—	.2	—	96.7
Indirect	.8	.8	.6	.4	.4	—	.2	3.3
Total	72.4	3.7	22.6	.4	.4	.2	.2	100.0
14 Textile-Leather								
Direct	51.5	2.1	41.0	—	—	—	—	94.7
Indirect	2.1	—	2.1	—	1.0	—	—	5.3
Total	53.6	2.1	43.1	—	1.0	—	—	100.0
21 Total Mfrg.								
Direct	34.7	26.0	12.7	4.4	—	.3	.3	78.4
Indirect	7.3	6.7	3.9	1.5	1.5	.2	.6	21.6
Total	42.0	32.7	16.6	5.9	1.5	.5	.9	100.0
22 Agriculture, Etc.								
Direct	10.1	—	24.5	—	—	.2	—	34.9
Indirect	26.2	3.8	31.1	1.3	1.5	.6	.6	65.1
Total	36.3	3.8	55.6	1.3	1.5	.8	.6	100.0
23 Contract Constrn.								
Direct	—	.3	—	31.1	49.6	—	19.0	100.0
Indirect	—	—	—	—	—	—	—	—
Total	—	.3	—	31.1	49.6	—	19.0	100.0
24 Transpn., Comm., Public Utilities								
Direct	34.1	2.3	35.7	—	—	3.1	—	75.2
Indirect	8.3	5.8	6.3	1.9	1.8	.1	.6	24.8
Total	42.4	8.1	42.0	1.9	1.8	3.2	.6	100.0
25 Wholesale Trade								
Direct	19.2	.5	42.9	.06	—	.6	—	63.3
Indirect	9.3	7.0	5.6	5.3	6.8	.1	2.6	36.7
Total	28.5	7.5	48.5	5.36	6.8	.7	2.6	100.0
26 Retail Trade								
Direct	9.4	—	82.7	.1	—	.93	—	93.1
Indirect	1.3	.9	1.3	1.1	1.7	.02	.6	6.9
Total	10.7	.9	84.0	1.2	1.7	.95	.6	100.0
27 Finance, Insur., Real Estate								
Direct	16.6	.7	42.3	4.5	20.1	.08	.4	84.6
Indirect	4.7	2.6	5.2	1.1	1.3	.08	.4	15.4
Total	21.3	3.3	47.5	5.6	21.4	.16	.8	100.0
28 Services								
Direct	13.0	.7	71.0	.9	2.8	1.0	.1	89.6
Indirect	3.3	1.9	3.7	.6	.7	.08	.2	10.4
Total	16.3	2.6	74.7	1.5	3.5	1.1	.3	100.0
29 Government								
Direct	—	7.6	—	—	—	91.1	1.3	100.0
Indirect	—	—	—	—	—	—	—	—
Total	—	7.6	—	—	—	91.1	1.3	100.0
30 Total Sales								
Direct	18.6	9.1	37.2	3.7	4.6	10.2	1.4	84.8
Indirect	4.8	3.5	3.6	1.2	1.4	.1	.5	15.2
Total	23.4	12.6	40.8	4.9	6.0	10.3	2.0	100.0

Source: Same as Table 3.

41

exports to the Federal government sector. Indirect ties to Federal government purchases may be substantial because of the volume of subcontracting associated with government purchases. (One value of an economic base study is that it helps to pinpoint the over-all importance of the Federal government in the community.) As a rule of thumb, only sales of prime contractors are considered as direct sales.

Finally, just as private pension receipts are included in Exports-private, social security receipts from the Federal government are included as income from Export-government.

Housing Investment

Housing investment can be roughly defined to include the local income earned directly and indirectly from the construction of dwelling units. Dwelling units may include multiple-family units as well as single-family units. Hotels, most likely, would not be included, but placed in the business investment category.

One possible classification of direct vis-a-vis indirect would place contractors and auxiliary services as directly related to housing investment. By contractors is meant those who work on the site. Such auxiliary services as architects, finance, real estate, and so forth, may also be classed as directly tied to housing investment. Indirectly tied to this sector are the materials suppliers and their suppliers.

Business Investment

The business investment sector covers both plant and capital equipment purchased by business in the community.[8]

Investment in business plant, like housing, assumes the construction industries are directly tied and their suppliers only indirectly tied to business investment. Business capital equipment is a tougher category to pin down. Machinery, desks, files and other such items belong in this category. The dividing line between an investment item and a current input is arbitrary. The important thing is to note what dividing line is chosen.[9]

State & Local Governments

Often overlooked in the discussion of Federal spending is the significant volume of expenditures by state and local governments. While there are some difficulties in summing up data for the separate governments, it does appear that some 10 per cent of the national product is spent by these units. In the future there is every likelihood that this share will be maintained or increased. For these reasons alone it merits attention as a separate sector.

From the point of view of a community, the sector includes all state and local government activities within its bounds. State and local government em-

---

[8] It is also desirable to define business investment by industries in the export sector as contrasted with local industries. If local industries do not grow proportionately, the impact on each type of investment will differ.

[9] The local income created per dollar of business investment in capital equipment is likely to be small since it is unlikely that any significant proportion of the goods used will be produced locally.

ployees belong in this sector. In addition, the output of firms which is sold directly or indirectly to the state and local governments is part of this sector.

Just as with business firms and consumers, it is useful to separate current operations from investment operations. Current operations of state and local governments involve the day-to-day activities of these units, e.g., police, fire, schools and so forth. Investment operations involve such things as roads, new schools, water mains, and other such capital goods expenditures.

One final decision might be involved in setting up this sector. Some Federal government functions within the community are quite locally oriented. For example, the size of the post office will depend on community size. Other activities also serve local needs, e.g., field offices of various agencies. Thus, it may be desirable to classify these in with the state and local government sectors.

Chapter 5

Measuring the Local Economy

This chapter discusses the measurement problems in carrying out a base study. The over-all test of a base study's quality is how well the data developed actually measure the base. But to this test should be added the qualifier, "at reasonable cost" because research funds are limited. In many cases where it seems that the quality of data can be improved, the cost is the restraint. In what follows it is assumed that the research budget is small.

The chapter begins by examining the various units which might measure the base. Next, measures which rely on existing data are discussed. Finally, the techniques for developing data through surveys are considered.

Units of Measurement

There is no single most appropriate unit of measurement of the economic base. Income, employment, value added, sales, and possibly some others, all can be appropriate units. Which unit one chooses depends on the purposes of the study and available data. It is necessary, however, to understand the conceptual problems involved when one or the other unit is chosen.

One of the reasons why the unit problem is not more crucial than it is lies in the fact that all of the suggested measures generally move together. Usually, when sales rise so does value added, and employment. The problem is that they do not move in the same proportions and sometimes when the changes are small, they move in opposite directions. A look at some of the possible units will point up the differences.

Sales, used as a measure, record total transactions. Thus, indirect export sales of $2 million might be associated with direct export sales of $1 million. If everything is added together, total transactions amount to $3.0 million. Income, however, will be much less than this amount. Sales, in effect, double count. Suppose a manufacturing firm which formerly dealt directly with a retail outlet now deals through a wholesaler. Even if the total value of the retail sales remains unchanged, the total sales recorded will increase, i.e., to the manufacturer's and the retailer's sales are now added the wholesaler's.

In spite of the problems of double counting, sales are a useful measure. For one thing, most business firms are interested in sales forecasts. The markets they serve are dollar sales markets. In addition to firms, local officials whose tax sources include any form based on sales are also interested in sales data so that they can estimate potential revenues. For these reasons, at least, sales deserve consideration as a possible unit.

Value added can be roughly defined as the sales of a firm less the cost of materials purchased from other firms. The unit value added avoids problems of double counting, since the value of the cost of materials purchased from other firms represents the sales by these other firms. Value added by an industry is roughly equivalent to national income originating in this industry.[1] Hence, value added gives a measure of income in a community. Professor Leven's study of Sioux City used this unit.

One of the drawbacks to value added is that corporation income is included. But corporations are apt to have several plants, some inside and some outside the community. Hence, a problem arises as to how much, if any, of the profits are to be considered as community income. Solutions are arbitrary. This issue should not be overplayed, since it is only a minor problem.

Income accruing to residents consists of wages and salaries, dividends, interest, rents, and other forms of income. The residents' income can be defined as that reported for tax purposes. Residents can be taken as those so classified by the Bureau of the Census. This measure of income is closely akin to Personal Income at the national level and is not as all-inclusive as a value added type of measure. Nevertheless, it has the advantage of simplicity and avoids the problem of non-local corporation profits.

Employment is the most commonly used unit, in part, because of its availability. The single element of this unit is the job. The difficulty comes in determining how much of a job a person holds. A part-time employee has one job just as an executive who puts in extra hours. Further, some people have two jobs; i.e., "moonlighting" exists. Unless employment is adjusted by some measure such as hours worked, employment is not too sensitive a measure. As will be shown, it can be misleading in measuring short-run adjustments.

The mere fact that four possible units were discussed does not mean that a choice must be made of one of the four. The benefit of carrying out a study with more than one unit of measurement may be worth the added cost.

Indirect Measures of the Economic Base

Given the unit of measurement, such as employment or income, the first step is to allocate the total to the sectors specified. This can be done by actually going out and measuring the various sectors directly. Most often, economic base studies have sought to use indirect methods to measure the sectors. A review of these indirect techniques will indicate their advantages and disadvantages.

Most indirect measures use employment as a unit. For exposition, employment will be used here although the qualifications concerning this unit should be recalled. Further, almost all indirect measures are concerned with only the division between exports and non-exports; other sub-sectors are not identified. Three indirect methods are the most common: (1) the assumption approach; (2) the location quotient; and (3) a variation on the second, the minimum requirements technique. Each will be considered in turn.

The Assumption Approach

The assumption approach is the simplest. An arbitrary assumption is made as to what is export and what is local employment. The usual assumption is that

---

[1] For a more precise statement of value added and income originating, see U. S. Department of Commerce, *1958 Census of Manufactures.*

all manufacturing and agriculture is export and the rest is local. This has been done, and it is attractive because of its simplicity.

The error involved in such an assertion can be enormous. A good deal of the manufacturing industry's products are locally oriented. For example, bakeries, printing and publishing, and brick manufacturing industries are classified as manufacturers. Yet the markets they serve are largely local. On the other hand, many services are non-locally oriented such as home offices of insurance companies. In addition, the larger the region, the more likely that a large portion of the manufacturing industry will serve the local market. This approach need not be considered any further.

Location Quotients

Location quotients provide one rather widely used measure of the export industry. Sometimes they are called coefficients of localization or specialization. When used to measure export magnitudes, however, the technique is the same. The underlying notion is simple. If a given community is highly specialized relative to the nation in the production of a particular commodity, the product is presumed to be an export item, e.g., automobiles from Detroit.

For a given community, start with employment during some year by industry groups. Then assume that the local residents have the same demand patterns that prevail on a national level. Take any industry, chemicals, for example. If the local community is self-sufficient in this product and neither exports nor imports chemicals, how much local employment is expected in this industry? The answer is the same proportion of total employment as for the nation as a whole. If 2 per cent are employed nationally, then expected employment locally in chemical industries is 2 per cent. In other words, just enough local employment to service local needs.

Suppose another local industry such as apparel has three times the proportion of total employment locally that it has nationally. In this case, the community is specialized in apparel and exports two-thirds of its output. Why are exports assumed to be only two-thirds? One-third is assumed necessary to satisfy local demands.

Finally, some industries in the community will show less employment than the national proportion. Here the presumption is that these products are imported into the community.

The location quotient method works by the following formula, or a variation of it:

$$\frac{X}{\text{total local employment}} = \frac{\text{national employment in industry } i}{\text{total national employment}}$$

Solving for X determines the numbers which would be employed in industry i in the community if it had just enough to supply its own needs. Assume X = 5,000 employees. Suppose that actually 12,000 were employed in industry i in the community. Thus, it is assumed that the 7,000 extra employees owe their jobs to the export market. The remaining 5,000 employees are assigned to the non-basic (local) sector. If this process is repeated for each local industry and the results summed, all employment will be assigned either to basic or non-basic sectors.

This location quotient technique has received much criticism in the professional journals. Many of the criticisms are justified. Some are not. Let's review these and see how the location quotient technique fares on balance.

The first criticism challenges the assumption of uniform demand throughout the nation. It is argued that the residents of one community may have different tastes than those in other communities, e.g., Southern California males just do not wear hats; West Virginians drink a good deal of soda pop; and pretzels are popular in Philadelphia. To some extent these variations can be taken into account. Data on consumer expenditures for many areas are available. Although it is true that these are broken down by the products people buy and it is difficult to trace them to the producing industry, nevertheless, some adjustment can be made.

A second frequent criticism arises from the question: What if the community is more productive than the national average in terms of output per employee? If this is the case, even with only the proportionate share of employees in an industry, the output is higher. In turn, some of the employment should belong in the export category. In the maufacturing industry, where this criticism is most applicable, an adjustment can be made. The *Census of Manufacturers* has data on value added and employment. Thus, an index of productivity, value added per employee, can be developed and used to weight local employment.

The final criticism is more difficult to deal with. The result one gets using location quotients depends upon the S.I.C. digit level used. What does this mean? Recall that industries are classified in various digit levels, the more digits the finer the detail. Suppose a community specialized in building run-about motorboats. This is part of the transportation equipment industry, S.I.C. 37. If location quotients are used at the two-digit level, no exports of boats may appear. Why? Because also in S.I.C. 37 are the automotive, aircraft, railroads, bicycles and other transportation equipment industries. The community imports these and so for the transportation equipment industry as a whole no exports appear. In fact, no exports may appear until the data gets down to S.I.C. 3732 — the boat building and repairing industry. Thus, the level of exports depends on the digit level used. Since there is no ultimate digit level conceptually, except the individual product of the individual firm, this is a qualification to be noted.

This final criticism has been given the label of the "problem of product mix." Product mix suggests that within any industry, even at a rather fine digit level, many different products are involved. Even a simple commodity such as aspirin has enough different brands to give one a headache. For even if a community produces an output of aspirin just sufficient to meet its own needs, chances are that it may be one brand. If so, probably a good portion is exported and other brands are imported.

Product mix, then, tends to understate the volume of exports. Table 10 compares the estimate of export-using location quotients with an estimate derived from a direct survey. Note that in every case location quotients yield a lower estimate of export levels. If one knew by how much location quotients are too low, then a correction should be made. But one does not know.

All of these criticisms reduce the value of the location quotient method. But they do not eliminate it entirely. For, on the positive side, it takes care of indirect as well as direct exports. A community with a large number of packing plants is also likely to have a large number of tin can manufacturers. Even though the cans are locally sold, they are indirectly tied to exports. Location quotients will show tin cans as exports and, thus, they do measure indirect exports.

Another advantage of the location quotient method is that it is an inexpensive way to measure exports. Sometimes there are not enough funds or time for more extensive methods. Moreover, it can be applied to historical data to reveal trends. As long as the limitations are recognized, location quotients can at least give some estimate, most likely a low one, of export levels.[2]

Table 10
Comparison of Export Percentages Based on Survey Results and Location Quotients, 1955-56
(S = percentage based on survey results)
(LQ = percentage based on location quotients)

Manufacturing*	Decatur		Ft. Wayne		Waterloo		Flint		Madison		Indianapolis	
	S	LQ	S	LQ	S	LQ	S	LQ	S	LQ	S	LQ
Food	87	71	67	26	91	83	—	—	92	71	63	24
Chemicals	98	44	—	—	—	—	—	—	—	—	100	50
Printing	—	—	—	—	—	—	—	—	—	—	51	24
Primary Metals	97	20	99	20	—	—	—	—	—	—	99	0
Fabricated Metals	—	—	—	—	—	—	98	44	—	—	98	11
Non-elec. Machinery	97	74	91	40	99	87	—	—	96	0	98	38
Electrical Machinery	—	—	99	87	—	—	100	81	99	0	100	67
Transportation Equip.	100	45	100	68	—	—	100	93	—	—	100	68

*Data are shown only for industries which are relatively important in the particular metropolitan area.
Source: Supplied by Federal Reserve Bank, Chicago.

Minimum Requirements Technique

A variation on the location quotient method is the minimum requirements technique.[3] The essential steps involved begin with a consideration of, say, 100 communities similar to the one under study. For each community, calculate the per cent of the total labor force employed in each industry. Rank the percentages for a given industry in decreasing order of magnitude. Thus, for example, 4.2 per cent of total employment in community 43 might be the highest for the baking industry. The next highest per cent in baking may be community 83 with 4.1 per cent. And, finally, community 14 has the smallest per cent, only .7 per cent employed in baking. (Clearly these are illustrative, not "real world" examples.) The presumption is that .7 per cent is the minimum required by any community to satisfy its own needs. Therefore, all employment in other communities above this amount is considered as export employment. Repeating this process for each and every industry yields total exports for the particular community under study.

---

[2] Location quotients have also been used to estimate what geographic export markets are served, state, regional, or national. Cf. George Hildebrand and Arthur Mace, "The Employment Multiplier in an Expanding Industrial Market: Los Angeles County, 1940-47," *Review of Economics and Statistics,* XXXII (June 1950), pp. 241-49.

[3] Cf. Edward L. Ullman and Michael F. Dacey, "The Minimum Requirements Approach to the Urban Economic Base," Papers and Proceedings, *Regional Science Association,* VI (1960), pp. 175-194.

Some have argued that with as many communities as 100, some oddballs may be involved; i.e., some whose location or economic base has quirks that are atypical. Therefore, do not take the per cent employed by the lowest community on the list. Instead, count up five communities from the bottom and use that as a benchmark. Of course, there is nothing magic about the 5 per cent level, but it avoids, supposedly, some spurious cases.

The difficulty with this approach is: Where does one place the cutoff point? The higher the cutoff place, the less each community will have as exports. Thus unless good judgment is used, this approach can be misleading.

Direct Measurement of the Sectors

The limitations of indirect measures of the export sector are sufficient to give pause. When they have sufficient funds, some communities have gone at the problem directly. And, while the direct methods are numerous, not too much liberty is taken if the efforts are placed in one of two groups: (1) the direct measurement of commodity and money flows from various sources of data; and (2) surveys of consumers and firms. Given the present state of available data, no attempt will be made to hide a preference for the latter. Yet direct measurement of commodity and money flows does have some merit, as will be shown.

Measuring Commodity and Money Flows

Once the community under study has been defined, a frequent first approach is to visualize goods and services flowing across the borders. If these can be measured, the volume of exports will be known. (Needless to say, at the same time, the volume of imports can also be determined, and this is useful information.) The question is: How does one find out what flows in and out?

One place to begin is the transportation industry. This will provide information on the movement of physical goods and people. If all forms of transport, rail, truck, barge, ship, pipeline and so on, are covered, the total should give an estimate of goods and services exported. This involves not only identifying the products transported, but their value as well.

The big difficulty here is purely empirical. The data are scarce. About the best source is the I.C.C. Waybill data collected by sampling freight car movements.[4] The difficulty with these data are that they are not in dollar units and can only be converted into dollars with some difficulty. Further, for a small region where volumes are not large, some of the sample problems limit the usefulness of these data. If railroad data are less than adequate, trucking data are all but non-existent. Fragmental studies have been made, but the bits and pieces are not particularly useful. Other transport modes present the same problem. Thus, great difficulties are associated with this approach and it takes a good deal of imagination and digging to develop these data.

If the outflow of goods is difficult to measure, perhaps something can be done with the inflow of funds. Ours is an exchange economy. Exporters have

---

[4]Interstate Commerce Commission, *Statistics of Railways in the United States,* (Washington: U. S. Government Printing Office), published for various years.

to get paid and funds will flow in. Some efforts have been made along this line under the title of money flow analysis, although not for the specific purpose of measuring the economic base.[5] Again, there are some data problems still to be resolved. A lot of funds flow back and forth that are not related to the exchange of goods and services. So for now money flows studies can be marked down in the hopeful category more than in the operational category.

Surveying the Local Economy

The most direct method for getting the data sought is through personal interviews and mail questionnaires. Surveys are definitely in order for economic base studies and community economic studies in general. Surveying requires some knowledge of how to go about it. The source of the sample, the sample's randomness and stratification, questionnaire design, pre-tests, levels of statistical significance and other technical matters require attention. These are beyond the scope of this discussion.[6] While all of the ins and outs of surveying cannot be spelled out, it is possible to indicate how surveys can help in an economic base study.

Basically, there are two groups from whom information is desired, people and firms. Let's begin with surveys of people, the residents of the community. The best way to get information on residents is to interview them. One of the pieces of desired information relates to the total income of the family and where it was earned geographically. Properly approached via a personal interview most residents are willing to reveal this information. (Experience indicates that mail questionnaires are unsatisfactory where personal data are required.) At the same time that income information is gathered, other information concerning local consumption spending, and attitudes about the community can be obtained. Thus personal interviews pay off in more than one direction.

Surveys of firms are also in order. In some ways they are more difficult than surveys of people, in other ways less so. One problem in surveying firms is that the same questionnaire does not apply to all industries. One can, for example, ask a manufacturer about his sales, but what are the sales of a bank? A department store may be able to estimate where its customers live and divide sales into export and local. What does the telephone company do? Are incoming or outgoing long-distance calls export, if either? Further, some firms have more than one establishment. A manufacturer of tin cans may also have a paper container plant. These need to be identified separately. In light of these observations, three points emerge: (1) design questionnaires appropriate to each industry; (2) decide, industry by industry, whether or not to use mail questionnaires; and (3) provide for multi-plant firms.

Some industries will require personal interviews. Not only will this help to insure a response, but any questions relating to that industry can be cleared up, such as the definition assigned to it. Other industries, such as manufacturing, can

---

[5] Cf. Norman Boshwer, Dewey Duane, and Robert Einzig, "The Flow of Funds Between Regions of the United States," *Papers and Proceedings, Regional Science Association,* III (1957), pp. 139-159.

[6] For a good expository illustration of economic surveys of consumers, see "Methods of the Survey of Consumer Finances," *Federal Reserve Bulletin,* XXXVI (July, 1950) pp. 795-809.

Figure 1

Area—SIC Code Number ....
Los Angeles-Long Beach Metropolitan Area

CALIFORNIA MARKETS QUESTIONNAIRE
(Rough estimates are acceptable for all questions.)

NOTE: This questionnaire applies only to the sales of the establishment(s) of your firm located in the Los Angeles-Long Beach Metropolitan Area.

1. Please describe briefly the major groups of products of your establishment(s):

....

....

IN THE FOLLOWING QUESTIONS, IF YOU SELL TO WHOLESALERS PLEASE DISREGARD THIS FACT AND ESTIMATE WHERE YOUR WHOLESALER SELLS YOUR PRODUCT.

2. First, consider your total sales this past year as going to two types of customers:

> (2a) those located outside of the Los Angeles-Long Beach area (see definitions) plus all sales to the federal government.
> (2b) those located inside of the Los Angeles-Long Beach area.

Estimate your sales between these two groups:

Percentages

(2a) Percentage sold outside plus federal government	36.1%
(2b) Percentage sold inside.	63.9%
	Total 100.0%

3. Taking a typical dollar of sales this past year estimated in 2a (outside plus federal government), how would you distribute this dollar of sales among the following two groups?

(3a) sales to federal government	26.2%
(3b) sales to other than federal government	73.8%
	Total 100.0%

4. Taking a typical dollar of sales this past year estimated in 3b (outside of the Los Angeles-Long Beach area and excluding the federal government), how would you distribute this dollar of sales among the following four areas?

(4a) sales to San Francisco-Oakland area	x x x
(4b) sales to the rest of California (omitting sales to Los Angeles-Long Beach and San Francisco-Oakland)	x x x
(4c) sales to the rest of the United States	x x x
(4d) sales to foreign nations	x x x
	Total 100.0%

5. Taking a typical dollar of sales this past year estimated in 2b (inside the Los Angeles-Long Beach area), how would you distribute this dollar of sales among the following four groups?

(5a) sales directly to consumers (people) which do not go through retail outlets	3.0%
(5b) sales to state and local governments	2.5%
(5c) sales to Los Angeles-Long Beach firms of capital goods; i.e., machinery and equipment	10.2%
(5d) sales to Los Angeles-Long Beach firms of non-capital goods	84.3%
	Total 100.0%

52

6. **Taking a typical dollar of sales this past year** estimated in 5d (non-capital goods to local firms), how would you distribute this dollar of sales among the following Los Angeles-Long Beach industries? ....

(6a) agricultural industries	
(6b) construction firms	5.0%
(6c) retail firms	1.5%
(6d) manufacturing firms	93.5%
(6e) finance insurance, and real estate firms	
(6f) other (please specify)	

Total 100.0%

7. **Taking a typical dollar of sales this past year** estimated in 6d (to manufacturing firms), how would you distribute this dollar of sales among the following Los Angeles-Long Beach industries?

Ordnance products	1.5%
Food and tobacco products	
Textile mill products	
Apparel and other garment products	
Lumber and wood products, except furniture	
Furniture and fixtures	6.2%
Paper and paper products	.8%
Printing and publishing industries	
Chemical products, including, drug, plastics, soaps, and fertilizers	
Petroleum refining industries	4.6%
Rubber products	
Leather and leather products	
Stone, clay and glass products	
Primary metal industries (e.g., foundries, steel plants)	3.8%
Fabricated metal products, except ordnance, machinery, and transportation equipment	47.1%
Machinery, except electrical	19.7%
Electrical machinery, equipment and supplies	5.4%
Transportation equipment (vehicle, aircraft, boats, railroad equipment)	9.9%
Professional, scientific and control instruments; photographic and optical goods; watches and clocks, etc.	1.5%
Manufacturing industries not covered in the above	

Total 100.0%

8. In order to give us some idea of the size of the establishment(s) covered by this questionnaire, would you please indicate the approximate number of people you employ: 100

AREA DEFINITIONS —
  Los Angeles-Long Beach Metropolitan Area includes Los Angeles and Orange Counties.
  San Francisco-Oakland Metropolitan Area includes Alameda, Contra Costa, Marin, San Francisco, San Mateo, and Solano Counties.

OTHER DEFINITIONS —
  Sales is the total dollar volume of your firm's sales.
  Capital Goods includes machinery and equipment, with a life of more than one year, used to produce other products.
  Non-Capital Goods includes all other products, excluding capital goods.

be surveyed by mail. Among the academic profession, mail questionnaires are not looked on with the same enthusiasm as personal interviews. There is merit to this caution. In this case, however, not too much is to be gained by a personal interview, aside from assuring responses from large firms. Statistical information is desired, not a depth interview probing for attitudes.

What kind of information is sought in these mail or personal interview questionnaires? Given the unit sales, or its equivalent for such institutions as banks, insurance companies, and so forth, the objective is to trace these sales to the sectors and industry groups used in the study, as in Table 8 in Chapter 4, where sales were traced to sectors and industry groups in Los Angeles. Figure 1 reproduces the questionnaire used in that study's survey of manufacturers and adds some hypothetical answers. While this is not the ultimate in questionnaire design, it does illustrate one method of developing the information needed. Particularly relevant are questions 2, 3 and 5.[7] Note that question 2 allocates sales inside or outside of the Los Angeles area. Question 3 identifies outside sales as either private exports or exports to the Federal government. (Question 4 merely distributes the private exports geographically.) Question 5 identifies direct sales to local sectors. From (5a) the local consumption sector can be derived. The answer to (5b) provides the information on the government sector. Capital goods, the business investment sector, are determined from (5c). (The housing investment sector is not included since manufacturers cannot deal *directly* with this sector, but only through the construction industry.) Now, the only sales that are left are to (5d). Where did these go? Questions 6 and 7 allocate these remaining sales. Question 8 gives the employment needed for weighting purposes.

Suppose an average firm, with 100 employees, in the Primary Metals industry, had answered this questionnaire with the figures as shown. These answers would supply the information necessary to complete Table 7 in Chapter 4. For example, 100 employees x 36.1% (2a) x 26.2% (3a) = 9.5%, the entry in Column 2, Exports Government.

Note that for the purposes at hand it is not necessary even to ask total sales. The whole approach can be in percentages. This avoids any queasiness firms might have about revealing total sales. It is necessary to determine the firm's total employment — which they seem more willing to reveal.

With employment as the weights, firm responses can be summed into industry responses. Given published information on industry sales, income and employment, industry information can be derived.[8] Finally, by the process described in Chapter 4, iteration, the sales can be allocated as direct or indirect sales to the various sectors. Thus, the sectors can be measured.

Measurements, of course, can have varying degrees of reliability. Hence it is appropriate to ask, what determines the reliability of the estimates? One factor is the accuracy with which firms fill out the questionnaire. While this is largely an intangible, the quality of the responses can be improved by pre-testing the questionnaire to uncover any difficulties and ambiguities. A second factor related to quality might be called the "community support level." If, through a

---

[7] Lest the statement after question 1—disregard wholesalers—leave a gnawing doubt that wholesalers are omitted, for the record they are not. It is simpler to treat wholesalers separately rather than try and trace goods to and through them.

[8] See Hansen, Robson, and Tiebout, *op. cit.*

covering letter and local publicity, firms are persuaded that this is an important undertaking, they are likely to be more careful in answering the questions.

Given the quality of the answers, the second factor which determines reliability is the response rate. How many firms respond and the total employment covered by these respondents determines the confidence of any estimate. It is particularly important to obtain replies from all large firms.

Without doubt this how-to-do-it discussion has left many holes. The only alternative to this brief discussion is a long list of step-by-step directions. But this would not help because there are simply too many variations from community to community for any one list to be meaningful. All that can be done is to suggest a general framework.

Chapter 6

Structural Interrelations in the Local Economy

The two previous chapters have shown how the local economy can be looked at in terms of industries serving sectors and how these can be measured. Implicit in that discussion was a theoretical framework of analysis. This chapter makes the theoretical foundation of base analysis explicit by considering the structural interrelations in the local economy. After a discusson of the long-run versus short-run time element in base analysis, a simple economic base "model" is developed. Finally, a fuller model is considered along with some of the conceptual issues of base studies.

The Time Factor in Community Studies

The discussion of community income and how the local economy can be divided up and measured has proceeded, so far, without a time dimension. Just as the local economy has been divided up at a point in time, it can be analyzed over time. Time enters in a twofold sense: the effect of the level of activity in one year on succeeding years, and the time span over which the study is to provide information.

The level of the economy in one time period in many instances influences the level of the economy in the following time period. By way of an example, note that the level of output in one year may affect the decision to invest in plant and equipment the following year. Today's consumption by families will depend, in part, on past income levels. When elements of this type are introduced, the analysis becomes *dynamic*. The advantage of dynamic analysis is that it permits built-in adjustments. Instead of long leaps into the future, more of a step-by-step process occurs. But there are difficulties. Dynamic frameworks, technically, are quite hard to handle. Further, they are chiefly useful in larger regions. This volume does not go into the details of such a framework.

The time horizon of a study is another matter. Here the division between short-run and long-run time spans is under consideration. Short-run time spans, as a rule of thumb, refer to periods from a few months up to around two years. Long-run analysis is usually concerned with five, ten and/or twenty-five year time periods. Sometimes, the distinction is made with reference to cyclical and secular changes. Cyclical represents the year-to-year variations as in business cycle analysis. The analysis of growth deals more with secular changes. In this context, the community which is concerned with the level of employment next year is asking a short-run question. If the community asks about employment ten years hence, its concern is long-run.

The Simple Base Relations

The first chapter illustrated the simple concept of the basic and non-basic dichotomy. Now, more explicitly, a "model" of the economic base can be developed which extends this simple concept.

The introduction of models in community research serves a useful purpose; major relationships are explicitly stated. Models involve groupings and statements about the relationship between these groupings. Naturally, models, like road maps, are abstractions. It is simply impossible to describe everything. The mere identification of basic and non-basic industries and the relations between them constitutes a model. By casting the analysis in the form of a model, the reader knows precisely what is assumed.

For exposition it is easier to consider first a short-run model and then a long-run model.

Assumptions: A Short-Run Analysis

Imagine that a community's economy has been divided into three sectors: exports, local investment, and local consumption. The unit of measurement is income accruing to residents. Thus, income accrues to local families from the three sectors mentioned.

Examples of such income would include: (export) wages and salaries paid by a toy manufacturer whose market is nationwide, wages and salaries paid by a local box manufacturer who sells to the toy firm, income received from the rent of a summer home to non-residents; (local investment) profit income of a local contractor, wages and salaries paid by a local cement plant; and (local consumption) income to a local barber, wages and salaries of the local ice cream manufacturer, the income of a dentist. The ties to these sectors, as the examples indicate, may be direct or only indirect. Finally, the interest, at this time, is in the year-to-year (short-run) variations in income levels.

In the short run, the level of income created not only in the export but also in the local investment sector depends largely on forces other than the level of local income. Exports depend on external market demands. The community is such a small part of this total market that it does not affect this market but is affected by it. Year-to-year variations in local investment are also assumed to depend on outside forces; interest rates, general credit conditions, and other such non-local factors. All of this means that, for short-run analysis, export and local investment income are taken as given, that is, they are measured but not explained by a base study. This leaves the local consumption sector which is "explained." What is meant by this?

The income derived from the local consumption sector depends upon local spending out of the income originating in the other sectors, just as non-basic employment was said to depend upon basic employment. In this sense it is explained. The nature of this explanatory dependency is important and needs examination.

The Local Consumption Sector

Income from local consumption is derived via a two-step process: (1) residents spend some of their income on local goods and services creating the sales dollars for local consumption goods and services; and (2) part of these sales dollars remain within the local economy and become local income.

Residents Spending on Local Consumption

What determines how much the typical family will spend locally on consumer goods? One of the most important factors is the level of current income. For present purposes other factors can be disregarded. The relationship between income and consumer spending is: the higher the income, the higher the spending.

Suppose that residents spend 50 per cent of their income locally on goods and services. Some of these goods and services may be produced locally like haircuts, while others are produced outside of town such as most items on a retailer's shelf. This can be called a propensity to consume locally with a value of .5. What do they do with the other 50 per cent of their income? Some is saved, some spent outside the community, and some is paid out for taxes. To keep things really simple, imagine a community where people always spend half (.5) of their income locally. Suppose dividend income (a type of export income) goes up one dollar. Does this mean that from this extra dollar of local income an additional 50 cents of income will be created through local spending? The answer is no, for there is a second component in the dollar flow stream which must be recognized.

Income Earned by the Local Sales Dollar

Not all of the 50 cents out of every income dollar that is spent locally is local income. Part of this 50 cents is paid out to bring in merchandise from outside the community (pay for imports), some may go as wages to non-residents, and to other such non-local sources. Yet, part will accrue as local income in the form of wages and salaries, profits, rents, and other such sources of local income. Suppose that 40 per cent remains as local income. If it is assumed that 40 per cent is a stable figure, .4 can be called the "income propensity of the local sales dollar."

This added propensity, when combined with the first, shows the relation between income, local consumption spending, and the local income derived therefrom. Out of every dollar of local income 50 cents will be spent locally on consumer goods and services and 40 per cent of this 50 cents, or 20 cents, *remains as local income.*

The Multiplier Process: Local Consumption

The added 20 cents of income through local consumption spending is not the total expansion of income. The "multiplier" process has not been completed. What does this mean?

So far, local incomes have risen — over and above the assumed one dollar increase — by an additional 20 cents. Part of this will be spent locally by consumers; in fact, one-half or 10 cents will be spent. Again, .4 of these sales dollars will remain as local income, 4 cents. But now local income is up by 4 cents and some of this will be spent — and on and on.

Fortunately, it is not necessary to trace out each round of spending and the local income created. A multiplier formula can give the answer more simply. The formula is:

1. Total Income Increase $=$ Increase in (Export plus Local Investment Income) $\times$ $\dfrac{1}{1 - (\text{propensity to consume locally} \times \text{income created per dollar of local consumption sales})}$

Equation (1) is much simpler than it looks. Use the above numbers and suppose again income from the export and local investment industries goes up one dollar. What is the total income increase? Since we assumed no change in investment income, the first term on the right hand side is the $1.00 from increased exports. That plus the two propensities yields:

2. Total Income Increase $= \$1.00 \quad x \quad \dfrac{1}{1 - (.5 \times .4)} = \$1.00 \quad x \quad \dfrac{1}{1 - .2} = \$1.25$

The multiplier value is 1.25. The original income change of $1.00 has been increased to $1.25 through the effect of the local consumption sector.

The more traditional base approach will yield the same result. Suppose that before any changes took place local income amounted to $125 million of which $100 million was basic and $25 million was non-basic. Now the base analyst is asked to measure the total income impact of just a $1.00 increase in basic income. Since the basic/non-basic ratio is 4 to 1, he would say that for every dollar of basic income another $.25 of non-basic income will be created.

If the base analyst wanted to be quite sophisticated he could use a multiplier formula as follows:

3. Total Income Increase $=$ Increase in Basic Income $\quad x \quad \dfrac{1}{1 - \dfrac{\text{Non-basic Income}}{\text{Total Income}}}$

Substituting the assumed values:

4. Total Income Increase $= \$1.00 \quad x \quad \dfrac{1}{1 - \dfrac{\$25 \text{ million}}{\$125 \text{ million}}} = \$1.00 \quad x \quad \dfrac{1}{1 - .2} = \$1.25$

This is also the same answer as derived through the multiplier process in equation (2). Since either method produces the same result as the multiplier in equation (2), why use the more complicated approach?

The advantage of the first formulation is that it points up the two propensities involved, the propensity to consume locally (.5), and the propensity of a sales dollar to become local income (.4). In discussing below such concepts as the stability of the basic/non-basic ratio this is important.

Short-Run Model Summary

At this juncture it is useful to summarize the steps that have been taken.
  (1) By definition, income of community residents accrues directly or indirectly from three sectors: exports, local investment, and local consumption.
  (2) In the short run, the income generated in the export and local investment sectors depends upon forces other than the local income level. To forecast these for the coming year requires information not considered here.
  (3) The income generated in the local consumption sector depends upon the local income level. Given the income forecasts for the export and local investment sectors, the income created in the local consumption sector can be forecast via this multiplier-type of process. The sum of the income created in the three sectors is, of course, total income.

Assumptions: A Long-Run Analysis

By changing only one assumption the above analysis can be useful in explaining *long-run* income levels; i.e., instead of forecasting the outlook for next year, what is the outlook for the end of the next decade? The assumption to be changed concerns the forces determining local investment.

Over a longer haul the level of local investment, and the income derived therefrom, tends to be more responsive to the level and rate of growth of local income. As local income from the export and local consumption sectors increases, new plant and equipment (consumer investment in housing can also be included) must be added in order to produce this additional output. Thus, along with a propensity to consume, one can imagine a propensity to invest in local capital goods. This can be introduced into the analysis in the same manner as local consumption.

The Multiplier Process: Local Consumption and Local Investment

Suppose the propensity to invest in new plant and equipment amounts to 20 per cent of income. In addition it must be remembered that not all of this local spending remains within the community. Some is paid out for imports of items needed for investment goods. Suppose this amounts to one-half. Thus, the propenisty to invest locally is .2 and the income created per dollar of investment sales is .5. These values can now be introduced along with the consumption propensities. The multiplier reads:

5. Total Income Increase = Increase in Export Income x $\dfrac{1}{1-[\text{(propensity to consume locally x income created per dollar of local consumption sales)} + \text{(propensity to invest locally x income created per dollar of local investment sales)}]}$

Substituting values assumed:

6. Total Income Increase = $\$1.00$ x $\dfrac{1}{1-[\,(.5 \times .4)\, + \,(.2 \times .5)\,]}$ = $\$1.00$ x $\dfrac{1}{.7}$ = $\$1.43$

The multiplier value is 1.43. It is higher than the consumption-only multiplier, given in (2), since both local sectors produce added income. Again, the advantage of this formulation over the more traditional basic to non-basic approach is that the assumptions and the economic mechanics are spelled out.

If the forecasted level of income increased earned in the export sector is $100 million at the end of the decade, income created in the local investment and consumption sectors will be up $43 million. In this sense, the model is useful in forecasting since only the level of exports need be given.

Forecasting Exports

A formula which forecasts the level of the export sector would complete, in a sense, the model. Indeed, to many base analysts this is the number one question. While conceptually a good deal can be said, at the empirical level things are less satisfactory. Because this topic is so important, the whole next chapter is devoted to it.

The Local Consumption Sector: Some Issues

In the professional journals debates over economic base analysis have covered a wide range of points. Before adding other sectors, the simple model with only three sectors — exports, local investment, and local consumption — provides a sufficient framework to discuss many of the points raised.

The most common debate target is the local consumption sector. In effect, the debates center over the local consumption to total ratio — whether the ratio is for income, employment, or some other unit. Five challenges have been issued: (1) for a given community the income derived from the local consumption sector is unrelated to total local income; (2) local consumption to total ratios are constant; no, they increase; no, they decrease; in any case you cannot be sure; (3) empirical studies prove the ratio is unstable; (4) the base formulation does not allow for import substitution; and (5) the ratio differs in different communities.

Figure 2

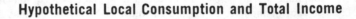

Hypothetical Local Consumption and Total Income

Low Correlation Case

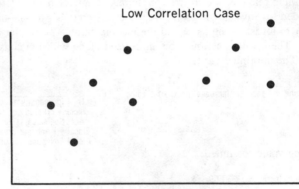

Total Income

The Correlation Between Local Consumption Income and Total Income in a Given Community

Proponents of the low correlation position argue that the proportion of total income earned in local consumption sectors is not closely related to the level of income. Because this issue questions the rationale of base analysis, it is desirable to begin by reformulating the issue more precisely.

In Figure 2 the low correlation case is illustrated. The various points in the graph are assumed to represent local consumption income and total income for various years in a community. No close relationship exists. Figure 3 illustrates the high correlation case. Here the observations for each year tend to form along a line. Knowledge of total income does help in estimating local consumption income.

Which of the two figures is correct? Again it is useful to recall the two components determining local consumption income: the propensity to consume locally and the propensity of a dollar of sales to become income. The first case rests on one of two arguments: either consumers' propensities to spend locally out of income are unstable or the income created per dollar of local consumer sales is unstable. That this is the essence of the argument follows from the local consumption multiplier discussed above. From one year to the next the value of the multiplier determines the proportion of local consumption income to total income. And the multiplier depends upon the value of these two propensities. So the simple thing to do is examine each propensity and see what reasons might suggest stability or instability. Direct evidence is lacking, but indirect evidence can offer useful insights.[1]

In considering consumers' propensities to spend locally it is useful to start with their propensity to spend in general, both locally and outside the community. Many factors other than current income add to the understanding of consumer expenditures, such as past income and family size. For a more refined

Figure 3

Hypothetical Local Consumption and Total Income

High Correlation Case

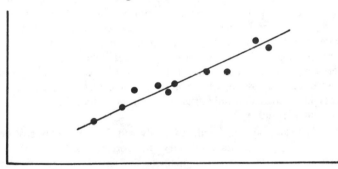

Local Consumption Income

Total Income

analysis these should be taken into account. Yet, subject to this kind of qualification, studies do indicate a stable relation between income and expenditures. What about the proportion of this spending which is local as opposed to outside of the community? If this proportion changes widely from year to year, even though total spending is stable, local spending will not be stable. Basically, this involves a question of geographical shopping habits. Here, marketing studies do suggest stability. The more isolated the community, the more likely this is to be true. A small suburb in an urban region would be more subject to structural changes; e.g., the opening of a new shopping center just outside the border of a suburb.

---

[1] Direct evidence would require local consumption income and total income for a given community that has been collected over time. To the writer's knowledge, no data of this kind exists.

This argues the case for a close relation between income and local spending. Now, what is the case for local income earned per dollar of local consumption sales?

It is easiest to visualize this issue by recalling that firms may be tied directly or only indirectly to the local consumption sector. Retailers, barbers, dentists, Good Humor men, and others deal directly with the local consumer. Bottling plants, local wholesalers, neon light repairmen, and others deal only indirectly with local consumers.

The existence of an "adequate" number of firms tied directly to the consumer sector is necessary if consumer goods and services are to be available at the community level. Adequate does not mean, for example, that one expects to find an opera house in a small Nebraska community. It does imply, however, that there will be no shortage of barbershops or gasoline stations. If local consumer-serving industries, for some reason, do not grow to accommodate a growing community, then consumers will readjust their spending patterns to importing more goods or saving more. The question is: Is it reasonable to suppose that local, direct, consumer-serving industries will grow with the growth of the community's income?

The evidence suggests that these activities do grow as the community grows, shrink as the community shrinks, and remain stable if the community neither grows nor declines. Perhaps the major reason is the ease of entry into consumer-serving businesses. In most cases, capital requirements are small. In turn, not only do new firms emerge, but existing firms are forced through competition to expand. The growth of food stores in the reader's community illustrates the point. It should be recognized that the growth of these consumer-serving firms does not take place overnight. Increased profits to existing firms act as a signal for others to enter, but a time lag is involved. Communities which have suffered a loss in some of their major industries can expect the process to work in reverse. Yet, only after time will firms find the local consumer industry unprofitable and leave.

The same sort of comments apply to firms only indirectly tied to the local consumption sector. Ease of entry, the forces of competition, and other such factors suggest that firms will adapt to the size of the local market. Again, with rapidly growing or shrinking communities some lags may be involved.

The four conditions necessary for a high correlation between the local consumption and total income can be summarized as:

1. Consumers' total propensity to spend out of income must be closely related to total income.
2. The proportion of the total spending which is spent locally cannot fluctuate widely.
3. Firms dealing directly with consumers need to offer a variety of goods consistent with the size (income) of the local market.
4. Firms indirectly tied to the local consumers also exist in numbers and variety commensurate with the size (income) of the local market.

The above arguments do not prove the high correlation case. They only suggest a high correlation. Their main advantage is that they specify the conditions which must be met. In turn, those who argue the low correlation case ought to specify which of the four conditions is unrealistic and not met!

Base Ratios

Up to now the question has been the correlation between the local consumption income and total income. Now the question is: What happens to the local consumption income/total income *ratio* as income in the community increases? Does it stay the same, increase, or decrease? In the jargon, the "base ratio question" is up for discussion.

Figures 4 and 5 illustrate three possible cases. Figure 4 begins with a simple local consumption income relation. This is Line 1. It is drawn such that local consumption income amounts to one-half of total income. Thus, in Figure 5 where the vertical axis measures this ratio, Line 1 corresponds to this relation. Line 2 in Figure 4 shows an increasing proportion of local consumption income to total income as total income rises. Line 2 in Figure 5 indicates the direction of this change, an increasing local consumption income to total income ratio as total income rises. The third line in each figure shows the decreasing proportion case. Fine. Now which one is correct? It depends.

A crucial factor in the analysis is how total community income changes. Suppose it doubled. Is everybody in the community twice as rich or does everybody have the same income, but there are twice as many people? In either case, community income will double, but local consumption spending patterns will be different. Even if the most usual case is a combination of both types of income change, it is necessary to understand this difference.

Figure 4

Local Consumption/Total Income Relation:
Three Possible Cases

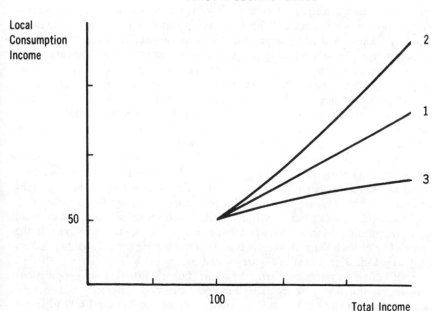

Figure 5

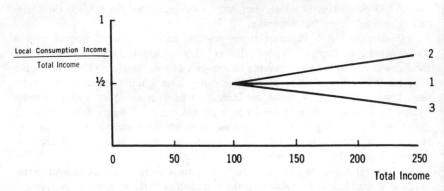

**Local Consumption/Total Income Ratio:
Three Possible Cases**

If the income grows because of population growth, what does this imply for local consumption income? First of all, the new residents are likely to have the same spending patterns on consumer goods and services — granting an impact on housing investment discussed below. This implies a need for more food stores, barbershops, dentists, and other such local consumer activities. The most reasonable expectation is that these will increase proportionately with the population-income movement. Hence, up to now Line 1 in Figures 4 and 5 applies.

Above and beyond this, however, with more consumers a market develops for specialty items: a legitimate theater, a local baseball team, a Japanese curio shop, and other such activities. Thus, consumers can now purchase locally items which previously had to be imported. An added impact comes at the indirect consumer level. With more food stores in the community, a local bottling plant becomes profitable and soda pop need not be imported. Added local dentists make a local dental supply house feasible. As economists put it, the size of the market is now sufficient in terms of economies of scale to support these new activities. *In toto* more, proportionately, is added to the local consumption income sector, Line 2. Less technically, the old saw applies proportionately, with growth "the city takes in more of its own washing."

The pure per capita income increase case is somewhat trickier. If people receive more income, their spending patterns will change. First of all, while they spend more in absolute terms, they are likely to spend less proportionately, taxes and saving taking a bigger portion of the income pie. A second factor is that such spending as does take place may show a relative increase in imports as opposed to local spending. More well-to-do families are apt to spend more outside the community on such things as vacations and clothes-buying trips. These two factors support a Line 3 argument in Figures 4 and 5.

Offsetting this tendency are the same factors listed in the population-income rise situation, new specialized stores, more firms indirectly tied to local consumption, and so on. In addition, higher income families are likely to spend more on services such as health, entertainment, and beauty parlors which are not only local activities but create more income per sales dollar. Thus, the two tendencies offsetting each other pull us back towards Line 1. Which is more powerful is a subject for investigation.

The combination of increases in total income due to population growth and increases in per capita income can, conceptually support any of the three lines in Figures 4 and 5. Thus, local consumption income may be an increasing, constant or decreasing proportion of total income as total income increases. Yet, to the extent that income increases due to population growth are the major element in any increase in total community income, the Line 2 position — local consumption income is an increasing proportion of total income as total income rises — is a most plausible expectation. Only repeated empirical studies can determine more completely if this notion is correct.

Unstable Ratios: "The Empirical Proof"

The niceties of the above argument notwithstanding, one seeming fact dominates the discussion: empirical studies do show that the base ratio is unstable and therefore meaningless. One such study can serve to illustrate the issue.

The Federal Reserve Bank of Kansas City looked into the behavior of basic and non-basic employment in Wichita, Kansas.[2] The relationship did not appear very stable. A score for the unstable side — or is it? Really, score one for the suggestion that employment is a less sensitive unit by which to measure the basic to non-basic ratios than income or other units. The reason can be simply illustrated.

Consider a merry-go-round owner-operator at the local amusement park. He will put in a full, but not very busy day, if unemployment is high in the community. Later, when employment picks up and people again take rides, his day will be busier and his income higher. In terms of employment, however, the owner-operator appears as one non-basic (local consumption) job at both times. If his income had been used as the unit of measure, the result would be more in accord with the reasoning behind Figure 3. Income changes affect spending rather rapidly and, in turn, the ramifications are likely to be felt quickly. Effects on employment, on the other hand, are likely to register only over a longer-run. Employment, then, as a unit of measurement is not too sensitive to short-run changes. As mentioned earlier in this chapter, caution is needed in using employment data to test the stability of basic/non-basic or local consumption/total ratios.

Import Substitution: A Neglected Issue?

Base studies focus a good deal of attention on exports, but say little about imports. Yet, it is clear that a community can add a dollar to its income by exporting more than previously or by producing locally goods and services which were previously imported. Import substitution implies producing locally some of those goods and services which were previously imported. Do base studies ignore this substitution?

---

[2]"The Employment Multiplier in Wichita," *Monthly Review, Federal Reserve Bank of Kansas City*, XXXVII (September, 1952), pp. 1-7.

Figure 6

Import Substitution: A Hypothetical Case

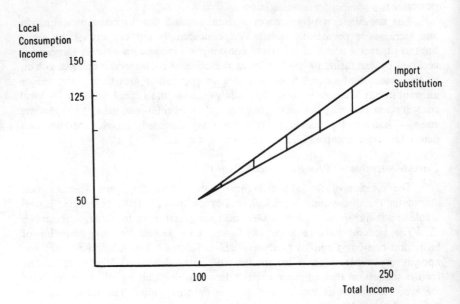

In Figure 6 a stable local consumption and total income relation is shown by the lower solid line. This particular line is drawn so that local consumption income constitutes 50 per cent of total income, i.e., the ratio is 1/2. When total income is $100 million, local consumption is $50 million. Now suppose the total income in the community increases to $250 million. If the income from locally produced goods rose proportionately, it would amount to $125 million. The presumption here is that more of the same goods and services are being produced locally. However, for the reasons noted above in connection with Line 2 of Figure 4, income from local consumption may rise more than proportionately as new unique stores and services are offered in the expanded market. Here, local consumption income amounts to $150 million, not $125 million. The difference, $25 million, represents import substitution. Thus, from an initial income of $100 million the vertical height in the shaded area shows the amount of import substitution at any higher level of income.

Economic base studies, in this sense, can account for import substitution. Of course, they do not account for import substitution which might occur because of technological changes, e.g., a new process makes local production less costly; changes in transport costs, e.g., it is now more profitable to assemble durable goods locally instead of importing the finished products; or other changes of this nature. Few economic frameworks can handle this kind of change. This does not mean they are ignored but simply that *after* a base study has been made these kinds of factors can be introduced in any forecasts of future community income.

Variations in the Base Ratio Between Communities

The final question is whether the base ratio varies from community to community? The answer is yes, but in a predictable manner. By the base ratio here again is meant the local consumption to total ratio in any unit — employment, income, and so forth. By predictable is meant that the variations can be explained on the basis of a few factors. Finally, by again looking separately at the two components of the local consumption sector — the propensity of consumers to spend locally and the local income generated per dollar of sales — the forces affecting the ratio can be systematically analyzed.

Several factors affect the prosperity of consumers to spend locally. A non-exhaustive list would include: community size, geographic isolation and income. Consider a large community vis-a-vis a small town. In the larger community, as mentioned before, more items are available on which to spend income locally than in the small town; e.g., opera. Studies of consumer spending, while not conclusive, support this notion.[3] Geographic isolation is a more apparent factor. Two communities may be similar in other respects, but if one is a suburb while the other is isolated, the suburb will have less local spending as more purchases are made in (imported from) the central city. Finally, as noted, higher income communities are likely to have a smaller per cent of the income spent locally.

The income generated per dollar of consumer sales also varies with the size of the community and its geographic isolation.[4] As communities grow in population the volume of consumer oriented activity grows more than proportionately as mentioned above. The degree of isolation is an important factor. If nearby communities can provide the indirect consumer goods and services, the market will be shared and less dollars will accrue locally per dollar of consumer sales. It would be surprising if Yonkers, New York, adjacent to New York City, had the same amount of indirect local consumer activities as Albuquerque, New Mexico, a city of the same size, but more isolated geographically.

Thus, the larger and more isolated the community, the greater the local income generated per dollar of local sales. Since consumers' propensities to spend locally vary in the same manner, the following general relation emerges: increased size and geographic isolation tend to raise the local consumption/total ratio. Or, stated another way, the non-basic/total ratio rises with city size and isolation.

Local Consumption Sector: Some Issues, Summary

In summary, the fundamental question to be answered is: what happens to the income earned in the local consumption sector as a proportion of total income? In base terminology, what can be said about the non-basic to total ratio, where local consumption income is equated to non-basic income?

1. For a given community, the correlation between local consumption income and total income is high.

---

3 Wharton School of Finance and Commerce, *Study of Consumer Expenditures, Incomes & Savings*, Vols. I-XVIII, (Philadelphia: Univ. of Pa. Press, 1956.)

4 There is a mutual interdependence between consumers' local spending and the availability of goods and services. These two components are treated separately only for purposes of exposition.

2. Empirical studies do not invalidate this notion, but suggest employment — as opposed to income — is not as sensitive a unit of measurement.
3. For a given community, as total income rises, the proportion earned in the local consumption sector may rise, fall or remain constant. Where the total income increase originates largely from increased population and employment, a rise in the proportion is the expected result.
4. Economic base studies do consider import substitution, i.e., local production of goods and services which were previously imported.
5. As between communities, the proportion varies systematically. The larger and the more geographically isolated the community, the larger the proportion of local consumption income to total income.

The totality of this argument is that the local consumption income/total ratio, or more broadly interpreted the "base ratio," is not subject to willy-nilly fluctuations. Positively stated, it is a meaningful, useful, ratio.

The Behavior of the Other Sectors

The discussion, so far, has shown how a three-sector model can be developed to explain income levels in the community in both the short and long run. Since the local consumption sector is so important, it was reviewed extensively. But what about the behavior of the local investment sector? How does it vary with different levels of local income?

The local investment sector is made up of three component sectors: local housing investment, local business investment, and local investments by governmental units. Each of these component sectors can be examined separately. In examining them the procedure followed in the discussion of local consumption is useful. The same two questions apply: (1) what determines how much is spent locally in each sector; and (2) how much of each dollar spent remains as local income? Consider these questions for each component sector.

Local Housing Investment

Local housing investment creates local income through the construction of single and multiple unit dwellings. In the short run, local housing investment may exhibit fluctuations not explicable in terms of community income levels. Stated another way, even with income constant over a two-year period, the volume of housing investment may differ significantly from year to year. Interest rates, downpayment requirements and occupancy ratios are factors which influence the level of activity in housing investment. For these reasons it is usually assumed that housing investment is not closely tied to the level of local income in the short run.

In the long run, housing investment is closely tied to community growth. For example, Table 11 compares the increase in Dayton, Ohio and Phoenix, Arizona. The two areas are of comparable size in terms of population and number of housing units. Yet, the rapid population growth of Phoenix has given rise to a greater increase in dwelling units over the past ten years.

Table 11

Dwelling Units in Dayton, Ohio and Phoenix, Arizona: 1950 and 1960

	Dayton Metropolitan Area	Phoenix Metropolitan Area
1960 Housing Units	212,796	211,865
1950 Housing Units	152,851	108,047
Per cent Change	Plus 39.2	Plus 96.1
1950 Population	518,642	331,770
1960 Population	694,623	663,510
Per cent Change	Plus 33.9	Plus 100.0

Source: U.S. Department of Commerce, Bureau of the Census, *Census of Housing, 1960, 1950; 1960, Census of Population*

Thus, like the local consumption sector, it is appropriate to think of propensity to invest out of income in local housing. Unlike local consumption, it is only appropriate in the long run. Moreover, the propensity to invest in housing is strongly affected by the *changes* in income as well as the *absolute level*.

What can be said about the local income created per dollar of housing investment? Will this vary widely from year to year? Most likely this proportion is stable. Much of the income is created by on-site employment — carpenters, bricklayers, and so forth. Indirect income is created in local product suppliers such as the local lumber yard and the brick manufacturer. How much local income is created indirectly is related positively to community size and geographic isolation. Larger communities probably manufacture their own vents, screen doors, and similar housing items. In smaller or less isolated communities, these are more likely to be imported.

Aside from its somewhat different behavior, there is another reason why housing investment merits special attention. The majority of urban land space is occupied by dwelling units. A necessary ingredient in planning and zoning decisions is some judgment about the total number of these units. Hence, an explicit recognition of this sector helps suggest the over-all total of land space required.

Business Investment

The business investment sector covers both plant and capital equipment purchased by business in the community. It is often considered as a separate sector for many of the reasons that housing investment is separated out for special attention. Students of business forecasting usually place a good deal of stress on investment at the national level. This is so, in part, because investment is an important cog in the income-generating machine. Beyond this, there is no simple formula by which investment can be predicted.

Business investment occurs when firms expect the investment will yield a profit. On a short-run basis expectations are determined by many factors in addition to local income. In the long run, local business investment is more likely to be related to local income levels. As the community grows, firms are induced to expand plant and equipment if they are to meet local demands. As with housing investment, business investment is not only affected by total local income, but by the rate of change in income as well. More rapidly growing communities would be expected to have relatively more income originating in the local business investment sector. In the long run, then, it is proper to consider a local business investment propensity related to local income.[5]

Indirect income derived per dollar of local business investment is likely to be stable. The income derived from expenditures on plant is larger than that derived from investment in equipment. Equipment is usually so specialized that little is made locally.

Finally, the relation of information developed with respect to business investment is useful to planning and zoning. Investment in business, like housing, utilizes land space. Some estimates of over-all totals, therefore, can be an aid in determining land use patterns.

Local Government Investment

Local government investments include items such as roads, schools, and water mains. Decisions to invest in these goods are made politically. From one year to another some variability can be expected. Large specific projects account for this variability. In larger communities, this is less likely to be the case. The over-all capital budget is less variable.

Over the long run, the size of local government investments is likely to be closely related to community income and its rate of growth. As total income and population expands, new schools, hospitals and other facilities are in demand. Even though the decision to invest in these items is a political one, the data suggest that this is closely correlated with total income and its rate of change. In turn, it is meaningful to utilize a propensity to invest by local governments.

The income generated per dollar of local government investment will vary with the nature of the individual projects.[6] In the aggregate, however, it should be a relatively constant amount, increasing with community size and isolation.

The three investment sub-sectors when combined into a local investment sector suggest that this single sector is related to long run income and rate of growth in a community. In the short run this magnitude is less explicable in terms of income. In turn, this discussion has given the rationale for the behavior of investment assumed in the simple three-sector model discussed above. In addition, the discussion has introduced three component sectors which can be

---

[5]The capital market is national in scope. Hence, the funds for local business investment need not come from local sources. This does not affect the propensity-to-invest concept. Regardless of the source of funds, as long as local business investment is related to local income, the effect is the same.

[6]The recently authorized Federal aid for public works in areas of high unemployment points up one reason why this sector is worth identifying. The impact on local income and employment of alternative projects may be an important factor in choosing among specific public works.

used in a more expanded model. Before introducing such a model, a fourth local sector should be added to account for the current operations of local governments.

Local Government Current Operations

Current operations of local governments include such day-to-day activities as police and fire protection, operation of schools, and provision of county nursing services. Like local government investment, changes in the level of these activities in the short run are probably not closely tied to local income. In the long run they are more likely to be. Unlike the local government investment sector, income derived from the current operations sector is less dependent on the rate of growth and more on the level of total income.

The income derived per dollar of current government spending is likely to be high. Most of these expenditures are for services where the wage and salary component is large. As with the other sectors, the income derived per dollar of spending can be assumed to be stable.

An Expanded Model

A seven-sector model as used in the Los Angeles study described in Chapter 4 can now be examined. Instead of three sectors, seven are used — Private Exports, Exports to the Federal Government, Local Consumption, Local Business Investment, Local Housing Investment, Local Government Investment, and Local Government Current Operations. But the basic formulation is the same.

In the *short run* all sectors except consumption are assumed to be determined by forces other than local income. Equation (1) given in the three-sector model reads:

1. Total Income Increase = Increase in (Exports + Local Investment) x $\dfrac{1}{1 - \text{(propensity to consume locally x income created per dollar of local consumption sales)}}$

With seven sectors in the short-run the only change is in the first term on the right side:

1a. Total Income Increase = Increase in (Private Exports + Exports to the Federal Government + Local Business Investment + Local Housing Investment + Local Government Investment + Local Government Current Operations) x $\dfrac{1}{1 - \text{(Propensity to consume locally x income created per dollar of local consumption sales)}}$

In the long-run more propensities are introduced. The appropriate equation given in the three sector model (3), takes the form:

3a. Total Income Increase = Increase in   x $\dfrac{1}{1 - [\text{(propensity to consume locally x income created per dollar of local consumption sales)} + \text{(propensity to invest in local business x income created per dollar of local business investment sales)} + \text{(propensity to invest in local housing x income created per dollar of housing sales)} + \text{(propensity to invest in local government x income created per dollar of local government investment)} + \text{(propensity to spend on current operations of local governments x income created per dollar of local government current operations spending)}]}$
(Private Exports + Exports to the Federal Government)

While this may appear unwieldy when written out, it merely summarizes the discussion above. A numerical example will be helpful. Assume Table 12 values.

Table 12

Hypothetical Propensities and Income per Dollar of Sales

	Propensity to Spend	Income Created per Dollar of Local Sales
Consumption	.5	.4
Business Investment	.08	.1
Housing Investment	.15	.3
Local Government Investment	.05	.2
Local Government Current Operations	.1	.7

With a one dollar increase in either Private Exports or Exports to the Federal government, equation (3a) would read:

3b. Total Income Increase = $\$1.00$ x $\dfrac{1}{1-[(.5\text{x}.4) + (.08\text{x}.1) + (.15\text{x}.3) + (.05\text{x}.2) + (.1\text{x}.7)]}$ = $\$1.49$

The multiplier value is 1.49 in this example. More important than the hypothetical number generated, the reader can see the logic and assumptions of this formulation.

Final Conceptual Issue: What are "Basic" Sectors?

The introduction of a multiplier-type of analysis and the concept of short and long-run time spans provides the answer to the frequent questions: "What are the basic industries of a community?" "Are exports the only basic industries?" "You mean to say that the only way a region can grow is by a growth in exports?"

The view of base analysis presented here is that *basic industries are those whose level of activity is not closely tied to the level of economic activity in the local community.* In the short-run, other sectors besides exports can be considered as basic; local housing investment is an example of one such sector. Over the longer time span only the export sectors appear as basic. The locally oriented industries will grow or decline along with the growth or decline of the export sectors.

Nothing here suggests that it is impossible for a community to grow without an expansion of exports. The world as a whole does not, as yet, export. Nevertheless, incomes have risen substantially. In like manner, an island community can increase its income even if it is isolated from the rest of the world. Increases in productivity and technological change are hallmarks of economic life. An increase in productivity of a locally oriented bakery will increase local income, even though exports did not increase. Nonetheless, this does not invalidate base theory. Base analysis, qua base analysis, does not focus on these changes. A base study, after all, cannot examine everything. All this means that changes in productivity, for example, can and should be introduced to modify any forecasts derived from a base study.

Chapter 7

Forecasting Community Economic Levels

This chapter considers how an economic base study can be useful in fore-casting. (It should be noted that an economic base study need not include a forecast and forecasts can be made without an economic base study.) Forecasting relates to both the short run and the long run. While there is much in common, there are distinctions worth noting.

Short-Run Forecasts

Short-run forecasts concern themselves with year-to-year variations in the level of income, employment or other units. What are the general methods of such a forecast?

Essentially, the method is to make a judgment about the level of activity in the several sectors and then see what this implies for the local consumption sector. By way of illustration, consider the seven-sector model of Los Angeles as given in Table 9 of Chapter 4. (There is no need to flip back pages, since no specific references will be made in this illustration.) Now imagine that seven business experts exist, one for each sector: exports private, exports government, local consumption, local housing investment, local business investment, state and local government current, and state and local government investment. Each one of these experts, excepting the local consumption man, has to estimate next year's level of activity in his sector — will it be up or down and by how much?[1] All sources of information are brought to bear. The housing investment specialist will keep his eye on such factors as occupancy ratios, interest rates, in-migration, and governmental housing policies. Others will prepare their estimates using information relevant to their sectors.

All of these estimates are then turned over to the local consumption man. His task is to see, via the multiplier process of Chapter 6, what this means for local consumption. Adding his result to that of the other six sectors yields the forecast of next year's economic level.

This above procedure is only illustrative and an oversimplification of the process. For example, some of the experts will want to adjust their estimates after seeing the forecast. If the forecast is gloomy, the local housing investment expert may lower his estimate. In turn, a new forecast will result.

---

[1] In what follows only a single forecast will be considered. In practice it is useful to forecast within a high-low range.

Long-Run Forecasts

Long run forecasts (5 to 20 years) involve much the same process as in the short run. The difference is one of emphasis. The export industries play an even more dominant role. Communities which have been unable to expand their export markets have not grown. Thus, major attention is on forecasting the export sector. It will simplify exposition if exports to the Federal government are considered separately. Here the interest is on private exports. As with short-run forecasts and the economic base itself, the discussion refers to studies with limited budgets.

Forecasting the Export Sectors

The most frequent, and perhaps most fruitful, approach is to begin by investigating the industries which currently make up the export sector. The current Pittsburgh Regional Economic Study, for example, recognizes that an important factor in community growth is the steel industry. Hence, one of their tasks is to investigate the future prospects of steel and its relation to the Pittsburgh area. The industries studied need not be only manufacturing groups. In Seattle, Washington, for example, wholesaling is an important export activity. Its future prospects will be of significance to the Seattle area. In fact, it is well to remember that manufacturing industries, usually the most sought after by developers of all industries, account for a declining proportion of national employment. Time spent on an analysis of future service export industries may be a wise investment.

Another technique is more difficult. At a conceptual level it is possible to ascertain the community's resources, its advantages and disadvantages and come up with some kind of economic potential. Against this are matched the needs of industry. Some industries will find the location favorable and others will not. Those who find it most favorable presumably will locate there and increase the export sector. What this amounts to is a look at location factors industry by industry, and a comparison of these with the resources of the community. When applied to a specific industry, these are known as "feasibility" studies.

The major difficulty with this procedure is the determination of industry requirements of material and service inputs. These are difficult enough for the products being produced today. But what about the products to be produced 10 or 20 years hence? Since the inputs are not even known, their locational needs are not discernible. Thus, this approach has limited usefulness without a substantial research budget.

A third method might be called the national share approach. The basic process involves three steps: (1) project or use someone else's projection of national employment levels industry by industry; (2) determine the share which your over-all region's export industries can expect; and (3) determine your community's export industries' share of the over-all region's total. (If the community is large enough, steps (2) and (3) can be combined.) The main technical problem is to determine the shares. Here again location factors come into play. In addition, industrial trends play an important part. Communities whose industrial composition contains a high proportion of nationally growing industries seemingly can expect a relatively greater growth rate. Unfortunately, predictions on this basis alone are not too successful, since other factors do enter in. Consider textiles and the South. National textile employment during the past decade has declined. What has occurred has been a redistribution in national textile employment favoring the South.[2]

One advantage of this share approach is that, if properly used, it allows a check on consistency. If a study estimates the community's share of national output at some future date, it also estimates the share of all other regions in the nation. By paying explicit attention to other regions, the study can see what shares are assigned to other regions. This implies that the community is actually seen as part of the total. All too often, community projections are not consistent. All communities see themselves gaining an increasing proportion of the national total. Explicit recognition that proportionately more for your community implies proportionately less for some other community is useful. It reminds the community that other areas also expect growth.

A final approach can be labelled a "business leaders' judgment" method. The idea is to tap the thoughts of executives of the leading export industries of the community. The presumption is that they are concerned about future developments in their firm and the industry. In turn, they are the most knowledgable about future levels of activity. The leading bankers of a community also will have a professional judgment about the future of local export industries. Interviews with such leaders or a conference with such a group could provide insights which would enhance the quality of a forecast.

All of these approaches seek to determine the employment in *direct* export industries. But what about industries *indirectly* tied to exports? Suppose the forecast includes an increase in the direct exports of electrical appliances. Associated with this will be an expansion of the outputs of other industries used as inputs by the appliance firms. Some of these inputs will be supplied by local firms which grow with the expanding export market. Other inputs will come from new firms which locate in the community. The remaining inputs will be imported. How much linked or indirect exports will develop depends upon the size of the local market and location factors. Suppliers do tend to agglomerate around an important industry, e.g., the automobile component firms in the Detroit area.

About the best place to begin in forecasting these changes is with the current indirect export industries. If direct export employment is expected to double over the decade, as a starter indirect export employment can be assumed to double — although this should be analyzed industry by industry. In addition, some new industries will develop in the indirect export sector. The same sort of location factors analyzed to determine direct export growth can be applied to the indirect sector.

As the reader is by now aware, these various approaches — matching local resources with industry needs, shares of national output, and industry studies — are all related. A feasible projection not only takes into account each of these factors, but many others as well. The hope is that some estimate of the magni-

---

2Cf. Harvey Perloff, Edgar Dunn, Eric Lampard, and Richard Muth, *Regions, Resources and Economic Growth,* (Baltimore: Johns Hopkins University Press, 1960), Ch. V.

tude of the export (direct plus indirect) sector can be made. Given this estimate, the non-export sectors can be forecast.

What about exports to the Federal government? How are these to be projected? Frankly, this sector is subject to a wide range of possibilities. All kinds of assumptions are possible from war breaking out to the attainment of a secure peace. Further, changes in the structure of government purchases of defense and space equipment will also have a differential impact on communities. If government exports are important to the community, about the most feasible thing to do is to recognize a wide range of possibilities and see what these imply for over-all growth.

Forecasting the Local Sectors

Forecasting the local sectors, such as consumption and housing investment, begins after the export forecast. Conceptually, there is no forecast involved. Given the estimates for the export level the level of activity in the other sectors can be determined through such propensities as to consume and invest. Unlike the exposition model in Chapter 6, these propensities probably are not simple proportions and some adjustments are required.

The only general comment that applies is that these adjustments require information gathered over time. What have been the trends of local consumption, housing investment, and other local sectors as the community has grown in size? Changes in community size will help explain variations in each of the local sectors over time. What is the nature of this relation? Can the influence of other factors, such as interest rates and changes in tastes, be taken into account? Like the export sector, research is required.

An Alternative Type of Forecast

For some purposes a forecast that is reasonably accurate for a large portion of the industrial structure may suffice. In such a case less costly methods may be adequate. If, for example, the objective is to forecast land-use needs at a future period, the following procedure may be adequate.

The past growth rate of total employment is projected to some time period in the future. For a large community historical evidence will indicate a high probability that its long-run growth rate will fall within a fairly narrow range. (This approach is not advisable for smaller communities where "random" elements are more likely to occur.) The underlying assumption is that the past growth rate for export employment will continue and that the growth of total employment will follow.

Suppose this kind of a projection indicates that at some point between 1977 and 1982 total employment will be 1,000,000 jobs. What can be said about these one million jobs? If the export to local ratio is 1 to 2, then 667,000 of these will be locally oriented and 333,000 will be export. At this juncture the industrial composition of the export employment is not known. It was merely assumed to grow to 333,000 sometime between 1977 and 1982. What about locally oriented employment? The industrial structure of the export employment does not affect the industrial structure of the locally oriented employment.[3] Thus, the structure of the locally oriented industries can be spelled out in some detail. It is then possible to estimate the land use requirements for each of the various locally oriented industries in square feet per worker or some such unit. This accounts for two-thirds of the problem. Only one-third, the export industries, are left to worry about. What can be done here?

The presumption with respect to the export sector is that its industrial structure is neither known nor can it be forecasted with a limited research budget. Yet two or three alternative export industry bundles can be developed with the existing bundle as a place to start. Each bundle has a different industrial structure which might evolve over the coming years. Before considering which one is the most likely, the first question is the impact on land use of each bundle. In the extreme it could be that all have the same land use requirements. If so, the problem is solved and land use requirements for export as well as locally oriented employment are known. The more reasonable prospect is that the different export industry bundles will require different patterns of land use. Yet even here, all that really matters are the differences between the bundles. Insofar as they have elements in common, part of the land use allocation problem is solved. Finally, with respect to the differences which still exist, a best judgment as to which bundle is most likely to occur combined with some flexibility in the over-all land use plan is appropriate.

The points to be stressed in this approach are: (1) the assumption of over-all growth from past experiences; (2) the allocation of locally oriented land use requirements without an extensive export forecast; and (3) the need to account only for the difference in possible export bundles. Certainly much more could be said about this approach, especially as to its limitations. As a possibility, however, it seems worth considering.

Summary and Conclusions

An economic base study is useful in forecasting community economic levels. Major attention in forecasting focuses on the export area and, subject to some qualifications, forecasts of other sectors can be derived from the base study. No specific forecasting techniques are outstanding at the expense of others and some plain digging is required.

What, then, has the economic base study really contributed to a forecast? First of all, it focused on the volatile sectors separately. Each was singled out for individual attention. Second, it insured consistency among the sectors. A base approach, for example, will not paint a rosy picture for local consumption if all of the other sectors looked bleak. Third, even if the forecasts are off the mark, one can check back and see where the errors arose. In time, with additional information, these errors can be reduced. But if the forecasts were made on some composite "judgment" alone, even though they might have been more accurate, they would still contain errors. These would be errors the analyst could not identify and later avoid.

---

[3] Admittedly this is subject to some qualification. For example, export industries which require a highly-skilled labor force will influence the choice of local consumer purchases; e.g., more cultural activities. Consumption data on communities with different industrial structures, however, suggest that these differences are not large.

81

Finally, and perhaps most importantly, accuracy in forecasts is not enough. It does policy-makers little good to report that expert judgment indicates an over-all 12 per cent decline in employment during the next decade, even though this expert judgment turns out to be more accurate than a base study forecast. An over-all judgment forecast does not tell you what sectors are in trouble and how they are related to other elements in the local economy. A base forecast is more specific in pinpointing the problem areas.

Selected Bibliography

The following list suggests some but by no means all or even a large part of the literature on economic base studies. Items were selected because of their readability and representativeness. A more extensive bibliography is given at the end of various chapters in Isard, *et al,* cited below.

General Background:

General background is provided by the chapters in any standard introductory economics text dealing with consumption, saving, investment and the analysis of income determination; e.g., Paul A. Samuelson, *Economics,* Fifth Edition (New York: McGraw-Hill, Inc., 1961), Chapters 12 and 13.

> The discussion of the Structural Interrelations in the Local Economy, Chapter VI above, draws heavily on a local adaptation of the tools of analysis of the national economy. Concepts such as the "multiplier," "acceleration" and "marginal propensity to consume" are more explicitly introduced in such texts than in Chapter VI.

Basic Text:

Walter Isard, *et al. Methods of Regional Analysis, An Introduction to Regional Science* (Technology Press of the Massachusetts Institute of Technology and John Wiley & Sons, Inc., 1960).

> The concept of the economic base as presented here on pages 189-205 is more restricted than ours. Chapters 4, 5, and 6 are especially recommended.

Articles:

R. W. Pfouts, Editor, *The Techniques of Urban Economic Analysis* (West Trenton: Chandler-Davis Co., 1960).

> This collection of readings includes many well-known articles dealing with the economic base. Several are especially recommended. Although technical and seemingly more critical than in fact it is, the article by Ferguson points up certain requirements for meaningful base studies. Blumenthal's oft-cited article criticizing base studies is included. These criticisms, it should be noted, are applicable to earlier oversimplified base studies. Alexander's base studies of Oshkosh and Madison, Wisconsin, are presented. The final three articles introduce input-output analysis and its limitations.

Charles Leven, "Regional Income and Product Accounts: Construction and Applications," in *Design of Regional Accounts,* Ed. by Werner Hochwald, Committee on Regional Accounts, Resources for the Future (Baltimore: The Johns Hopkins University Press, 1961), pp. 148-195.

Especially interesting is Appendix Table C and the discussion of it in the text. This table shows the results of a "to-from" study of Sioux City, Iowa, using value added as the unit of measurement.

George Hildebrand and Arthur Mace, "The Employment Multiplier in an Expanding Industrial Market: Los Angeles County, 1940-47," *Review of Economics and Statistics,* XXXII (August '50), pp. 241-249.

This is one of the best early applications of multiplier analysis to a particular area.

Richard Peterson, *The Economic Base of Sacramento,* Economics Department, Bank of America, San Francisco, 1961.

This non-technical study, which includes a projection for the Sacramento area, shows what can be done by a capable researcher on a limited budget.

Edward Ullman and Michael Dacey, "The Minimum Requirements Approach to the Urban Economic Base," *Papers and Proceedings, Regional Science Association,* VI (1960), pp. 175-194.

The minimum requirements approach, discussed in Chapter V, is well articulated in the article.

Edward L. Ullman, Michael Dacey and Harold Brodsky, *The Economic Base of the 101 Largest United States Metropolitan Areas and Minimum Requirements for 1960,* Washington Center for Metropolitan Studies, Washington, D.C., and Center for Urban and Regional Studies, University of Washington, Seattle, c 50 pages, forthcoming in 1968.

This study has 14 industry economic base profiles showing number and percent employed, export and local employment, for all U.S. metropolitan areas over 250,000 population in 1960, together with total population, percent change, unemployed, military, minimum requirement, and excess. The original minimum requirements study is also reprinted together with 1960 data and additional discussions and comparisons.

Benjamin Chinitz, "Contrasts in Agglomeration: New York and Pittsburgh," *American Economic Review, Papers and Proceedings,* LI (May, 1961), pp. 279-289.

This piece considers many supply aspects which help to determine the economic "environment" in a community.

Printed in U.S.A.
First Printing, December, 1962
Second Printing, August, 1963
Third Printing, February, 1968
Fourth Printing, August, 1970
Committee for Economic Development
477 Madison Avenue, New York, N.Y. 10022